W9-AAI-689

MANAGING
WITH
WISDOM

MANAGING
WITH
WISDOM

Jack H. Grossman

PELICAN PUBLISHING COMPANY

Gretna 1996

The word "Pelican" and the depiction of a pelican are trademarks
of Pelican Publishing Company, Inc., and are registered
in the U.S. Patent and Trademark Office.

Library of Congress Cataloging-in-Publication Data

Grossman, Jack H.
    Managing with wisdom/ Jack H. Grossman
        p.   cm.
    ISBN 1-56554-112-X (hc : alk. paper)
    1. Management—Psychological aspects. 2. Interpersonal relations.
    3. Self-management.   I. Title.
    HD38.G7618 1995
    658—dc20   95-31933
                                                                    CIP

Manufactured in the United States of America

Published by Pelican Publishing Company, Inc.
1101 Monroe Street, Gretna, Louisiana 70053

To all the people
whose daily acts of wisdom
make this world a better place
in which to live.

And to the very special people in my life
whom Joan and I lovingly call
"our family."

Contents

Acknowledgments 9

Introduction..11

Chapter 1   Marketing-Based and
             Personal-Based Relationships 17

Chapter 2   Dealing with Life's Problems 29

Chapter 3   Developing a Sound Relationship
             with Yourself 55

Chapter 4   Developing Sound Relationships
             with Others 97

A Few Final Words of Wisdom 159

Acknowledgments

People have asked me, "How long did it take you to write this book?" I answer, "A lifetime." My response is genuine, although it sounds like a philosophical answer to a concrete question. Yes, it has taken me a professional lifetime to formulate the ideas I share with you. And, as you might expect, the principles contained in this book were not forged in a vacuum, nor did they come together in this book without the help of people I wish to acknowledge.

First, to my students at DePaul University, my academic home since 1965, thank you for wanting to learn. Your perceptive questions and critical comments helped me develop many of the ideas contained in this book. As you know, responsive and intellectually stimulating students are essential if a teacher is to be effective. I appreciate your helping me to become the best teacher I could be.

Second, I acknowledge my corporate clients. Your challenging problems, those that affect the "bottom line," enable me to test the practicality of the principles and tools I discuss in this book. I thank you for trusting me enough to share your concerns with me and for allowing me to help you resolve them.

I extend my deepest gratitude to Connie Goddard, my agent.

During the early stages of this project, your penetrating questions and thoughtful comments helped me to shape my manuscript into a form worthy of publication. Thanks to your excellence as an editor and to the foresight of Carolyn Ferrari (formerly of Pelican Publishing Company), my original manuscript was transformed into *Managing with Wisdom*. The final touches to this book, those of my editor, Nina Kooij, are the marks of a professional. Thank you, Nina, for contributing your skillful editing to my work.

Finally, I offer an extraspecial thank-you to my lifelong friend and partner, Joan, whose unique brand of wisdom continues to be a constant source of inspiration and guidance to me, to our children, and to our grandchildren.

Introduction

While writing this book, I realized that as a society we are knowledge rich and wisdom poor. We know a lot, but frequently we either misuse our knowledge or we do not use it at all. One would think that, with all the "how-to" books that have been written on managing people, improving marriages, becoming a better parent, and becoming an effective leader, people would be more civil and effective in dealing with others. However, that is not the case. There is no evidence to suggest that the ideas presented and techniques touted in such inspirational and helpful books have had a profound long-term effect on our society.

Although knowing is generally a prerequisite to doing, it does not follow that just because someone knows what constitutes appropriate action, he or she will indeed act appropriately. Many of us do lots of things we know are wrong, and do not do things we know are right. Obviously, we need more than knowledge to be better than we are. We need *wisdom*. Whether your management responsibilities are restricted to your own life or include the additional responsibility of managing others, you can, with increased wisdom, become a better manager than you are. To help you do that is my aim in this book.

Wise managers—decent and respectable people who lead

productive lives—share one distinguishing characteristic: they *consistently* employ "common-sense" principles to achieve their desires. Because their intelligence is tempered with good judgment, they usually say and do the right things, in the right way, and at the right time and place. Their sense of what is proper and improper prompts them to make appropriate use of their intellect, knowledge, and experiences to accomplish what they want. That sense enables them to bring out the best in others much of the time and to get people under their influence to give their all willingly to a common cause. In short, they excel as problem solvers, teachers, and sellers of ideas—three functions everyone performs, regardless of his or her position.

Although some people are naturally endowed with the sensitivities and skills associated with wisdom, most of us have to develop those abilities. How? By learning the principles and tools wise managers intuitively employ, understanding why and how they work, and then practicing them regularly and long enough until they become an integral part of our management style.

The principles and tools discussed in this book can help you fulfill two objectives, which, once attained, will enable you to lead a more fruitful life, be a role model, and enjoy the status of "wise manager." Those objectives are (1) to elevate your self-respect, so you can gain greater control of your life, and (2) to build strong and healthy communication bridges that will allow you to connect with people you value, both in business and in your personal life.

The principles I share with you are outgrowths of thirty-plus years' experience as a teacher, counselor, and consultant. As a teacher at DePaul University in Chicago, I have been privileged to test and refine the principles contained in this book with classes that are a microcosm of middle- and upper-middle-class America. The classes consist of students differing in color, religion, sexual orientation, marital status, occupation, and position. Most of them have told me that they have seen noticeable improvements in both their business and personal relationships since taking the course on which much of this book is based. Their testimonials are strong evidence that the principles contained in this book work.

There is nothing magical, mystical, "techniquish," or trendy about these principles. Rather, they are practical, jargon free, and based on common sense, which is why they are effective. But, for them to have lasting value for you, you need to put forth effort. As thousands of my university and business students can attest, if you are serious about becoming a better manager, i.e., a better person, and are willing to invest the time and energy toward this worthy pursuit, you will gain the knowledge, skills, and wisdom to be the best you can be.

To gain maximum benefit from this book, do the exercises and projects recommended in each principle and keep them all in a special notebook. If a principle does not contain a project or exercise but stimulates thinking, find someone to discuss the principle with. And always practice the skills you want to develop.

Now, let me say a few words about the organization of this book. Since the nature of your relationships with people determines how you deal with them, the book begins with a discussion of principles governing two types of relationships: "marketing based" and "personal based." These principles will help reduce your disappointments in people by creating realistic expectations of them.

Following the discussion of these two types of relationships, and of how to gain maximum benefit from each, the book contains a series of basic principles and tools that will serve as your foundation for dealing with life's problems. Then, based on the notion that *you must have a sound relationship with yourself for your relationship with others to be sound,* the book provides principles and tools to accomplish that objective. The book concludes with principles and tools for developing effective relationships with other people you value.

Although this book is organized in what I believe is a logical order, feel free to skip around to whatever principles interest you. In so doing, you can, simultaneously, work on skills that have both immediate and long-term value.

Most wise managers I have spoken with have said that the secret of their success, both in their professional and personal lives, is to practice consistently the "golden rule": *treat others as you would like them to treat you* (or some variation of this). A rarely voiced companion to this rule is *treat yourself as you would like others to treat you.* My aim is to show you how to make both those rules come alive and benefit you.

If you do your part, you will see almost immediate results from your efforts. This I guarantee.

My best wishes to you as you journey toward the wisdom that will enable you to become the best *you* you can be.

MANAGING WITH WISDOM

CHAPTER 1

Marketing-Based and Personal-Based Relationships

The *primary* basis of any relationship is either "marketing" or "personal." Marketing-based relationships, such as those you develop at work or when you exchange goods and services, are rational and exist because of what people *do* for each other. Personal-based relationships, such as those you have with your friends and relatives, exist because of what people *are* or *mean* to each other; they are held together primarily by emotional bonds.

While many relationships are mixtures of the two, the core of all relationships is one or the other. The main distinction between them concerns the nature and extent of your expectations. Regardless of whether they are marketing or personal based, relationships may vary from 1 (poor) to 10 (outstanding) in quality.

To prevent or reduce unnecessary disappointments, you need to classify each major relationship as one type or the other, assess its quality, and know what you can reasonably expect from it. To help you do those things is the objective of these first three principles.

1. In marketing-based relationships,
you can give as much as you want,
but expect only what you contract for; no more.

Most relationships are marketing based in that the primary reason for their existence is business related, i.e., what these people can *do* for each other. The rationale for people's association in this type of relationship is that the parties provide concrete value to each other in the form of either goods or services. Relationships between employer and employee, professional advisors and their clients, store personnel and their customers, and people who work together are all examples of marketing-based associations.

In such relationships, people have an implied or formal contract concerning their mutual expectations. For example, since my association with my students is marketing based, we agree that I am there to teach and give them a grade for the course, providing they do the required work and abide by the rules they agreed to by signing up for the class. My expectations of them, as well as what they can expect from me, are clearly stated in a syllabus, which I give them at our first meeting.

Essentially, that's how it is with all marketing-based relationships; expectations are limited to whatever oral, written, or implied "contract" people agree to. Any expectations beyond the contract are illegitimate. This is not to say that both parties wouldn't like more than they agree to. Of course they would, but they don't have a right to expect more.

It would be out of line, for example, for me to expect students to thank me following an especially good class. Although it would be pleasant to receive thanks, if I expected it I'd set myself up for constant disappointment since that's not part of our agreement. Similarly, if students expected me to write letters of recommendation just because they were in my class, many would be upset with me since I will only do that for exceptional students.

When people with whom you have a marketing relationship extend themselves beyond the boundaries of your agreement, view it as a *bonus*. Bonuses are great, since they are like gifts and, therefore, wonderful, exciting surprises. I am thrilled, for example, when students voluntarily tell me how much they gained from a particular discussion. I am excited when I get a thank-you note from a former student telling me how certain principles discussed in class helped him in his job or in a personal relationship. I am gratified when a client expresses his appreciation for something I did that had a positive effect on his business. But certainly I don't expect those gifts.

Although your expectations of marketing relationships should be limited to your implicit or explicit agreements, you can give of yourself as much as you like. For example, with regard to my students, I will do almost anything to help them understand the principles I teach or to assist with some other school-related problem. But I don't expect anything extra from them. Similarly, well-run companies will go out of their way to provide excellent service and show appreciation to their customers, but customers are not expected to do anything other than be loyal and pay their bills.

The point: *What you do for others is under your control. But when you expect others to do something for you, you relinquish control to them. Therefore, to reduce your chances of being disappointed in marketing-based relationships, don't expect more than you contract for, either implicitly or explicitly, and enjoy whatever bonuses you receive.*

To determine which of your important relationships fall into the marketing-based category, ask yourself the following question relative to each person: "If it weren't for the things we *do* for each other as part of our business or professional association, or if we didn't work in the same organization, would we have anything to do with each other?" If your answer is "no" or "probably not," the relationship is marketing based.

Marketing-based relationships *formally* end when the "contract" is fulfilled or when one or both parties change work environments. Although these relationships could evolve into personal ones, that happens infrequently. (How to make successful transitions from marketing-based to personal-based relationships is discussed under Principle 3.)

Assessing the Quality of Your Marketing-Based Relationships

To assess the quality of each of your important marketing-based relationships, answer the following questions:

What holds the affiliation together, i.e., what do you get from each other?

Do you *consistently* get what you expect from the person?

Regarding the positive things you receive, but do not expect, how would you rate (on a 1-10 scale, with 10 representing the high end of the scale) the frequency with which you receive such bonuses?

(Using this same scale, answer the following questions.)

How much do you value the benefits you get from the service (or product) this person provides?

To what extent do you enjoy this person's company? How much do you like being with this person?

How much do you respect him or her as a person?

How much do you trust him or her with personal matters or with your personal feelings?

The more you and the other half of your marketing relationship do for and mean to each other, both as part of your "contract" and as people, the stronger the marketing bond and the higher the quality of your relationship.

You can do your part to strengthen your important marketing relationships by following the advice of Bill, a salesman I knew who was consistently the top producer in the distribution firm where he worked. When I asked him for his secret of success, Bill said, "I make it easy for people to buy from me. I not only anticipate their desires and fulfill them, but I provide them with whatever services they need to be more effective. And I do it in a way that makes it look like it's no big deal. My customers know that they can count on me to help them solve their problems."

What can *you* do to make it easy for your marketing-based relationships to give you what you want? How can *you* motivate people to extend themselves for you and give you bonuses? Your answers to those questions will lead you to actions that can improve your major marketing-based relationships. You might want to stop reading for a few minutes to write down your responses to those questions. (*Hint:* You have to give people what they want for them to give you what you want.)

As the quality of a marketing relationship improves, two things happen. First, the number of things people desire from and do for each other increases. And, second, they begin to develop a low-level personal relationship, which calls for them to do things with each other. One source of evidence that this development occurs comes from successful salespeople I have talked with. All of them have told me that a major strategy for generating business is to get their customers and prospects to like them. In so doing, even though the relationship is still marketing based, the emotional component of the personal relationship strengthens their marketing bond.

To improve the quality of all major marketing-based relationships, consider the following guidelines:

1. Know the other person's wants, needs, and what he or she expects from you.

2. Give as much as you reasonably can, consistent with the person's desires and expectations.

3. Extend your giving beyond the person's expectations. That is, offer reasonable bonuses, such as occasional invitations to lunch or dinner. If the person accepts your

bonuses, it indicates his willingness to extend the relationship beyond your "contract." However, if your offers are rejected, the person does not want to advance the marketing relationship beyond its current level.

4. Make sure the other person knows what you want, need, and expect. If at any time your needs or expectations are not fulfilled, let the person know specifically the nature of your problem. For example: "I have a problem. I thought we agreed _____. What happened?" Or "My understanding was _____. Was your understanding different?" That way, you are putting the misunderstanding on a discussion level.

5. When a bonus is extended to you, realize it is a person's way of strengthening your marketing-based relationship. When you can, graciously accept those bonuses.

Regardless of its strength, don't lose sight of the fact that a marketing-based relationship, by its very nature, is *conditional*. It exists because you and the other person value the things you *do* for each other, share the same work environment, or both. Once those conditions end, so does the relationship.

2. In personal-based relationships, expect no more than people are able or willing to give.

Your relationships with acquaintances, neighbors, friends, and people related to you by blood or marriage are personal based. Such relationships are primarily functions of what people *are* or *mean* to each other. The bonds may be legal, emotional, or both. What the people do for each other is secondary.

Except for our relationships with our spouses and other friends, we do not choose personal-based relationships. Yet, because they are all important forces in our lives, we are obliged to maintain them; that's the *least* we can do. The following three basic rules will enable you to fulfill that primary obligation:

1. *Honor reasonable minimal expectations,* such as attending certain family functions ("command performances") or making periodic "How are you doing and what's new?" phone calls. Or, if the person is a neighbor, fulfill whatever neighborly duties are required of you to preserve the relationship at the quality level you desire.

2. *Expect no more than a person is able or willing to give, and do not impose expectations beyond the minimum.* Although people in personal-based relationships tend to be accommodating, tolerant of each other's weaknesses, protective of each other, and forgiving, pushing expectations beyond a person's limits can weaken, if not destroy, the emotional bond of those relationships. Accepting people in this type of relationship for who and what they are will likely maintain it.

3. *While you may not understand the reasons for doing what you must to maintain a personal-based relationship, do it anyway.* For example, you may not understand why "making small talk" at family gatherings is necessary with people you do not like, but if that's what it takes to preserve those relationships, you would be wise just to do it. We don't have to understand the reason for everything we have to do. The fact that they accomplish our objectives is reason enough to continue doing them. Here's another example: you may not understand why someone close to you requires more pats on the back or encouragement than you consider "normal." But, again, if that's what it takes to maintain the relationship you want with that person, and it's not painful to you, accommodate that need.

Those three rules are essential for maintaining just the lowest-level personal-based relationships. But, when those relationships improve, they become more difficult to maintain because the rules and principles that govern them become more extensive and complex. To prove that to yourself, envision two of your very best friends—people who fulfill your ideal of what a "best friend" is and does. Now, keeping those persons in mind, consider the following statements and, for each, answer the question, "Is this behavior or attitude consistent with what I would reasonably expect from these two people?"

1. My friends accept me for who and what I am; they do not attempt to remake me into their image of the person they would like me to be.

2. My friends are physically there for me when I need them.

3. My friends are emotionally supportive when I need it; they rarely, if ever, judge my feelings.

4. My friends make it easy for me to ask for help or for favors when I need them; they do not cause me to feel guilty when I request help.

5. My friends feel free to ask for my help or for favors they want of me.

6. My friends share their joys and sorrows with me; I do not have to find out about them through others.

7. My friends encourage me to express my joys and sorrows with them; they do not make me feel guilty when I do.

8. My friends and I have similar values, which serve as the foundation for our relationship.

9. My friends encourage me to talk about my interests, even if they don't necessarily participate in them with me.

10. My friends and I have at least one interest in common.

11. My friends respect and trust me; they don't ever take me for granted.

12. My friends are trustworthy and fulfill their promises to me; they don't do anything that would cause me to distrust them.

A "yes" to all 12 statements characterizes the highest-level personal-based relationship, a "10" on a 1-10 rating scale. That being your bench mark for what you can expect from the best possible personal-based relationship any person can have, you can assess the quality of all your other personal-based relationships. Doing so will enable you to set your expectations realistically, consistent with the nature and quality of those relationships.

This exercise will provide you with two benefits. First, you will no longer set yourself up for disappointments by expecting things that people either can't or won't deliver. Second, and equally important, you can enjoy each personal-based relationship for what it actually is, rather than being angry or upset because it isn't what you would like it to be.

When Ed, a forty-nine-year-old department manager, devoted husband, and father of three married children, did this exercise, he was pleased that only two of his personal-based relationships rated as high as "8" or "9." He said, "I'm relieved because I don't have enough time and energy to be that close to more than two or three people." The point is, personal-based relationships that rate less than "8" are just fine and need not concern you. Actually, you would be better off if you kept your expectations to a minimal level with most personal-based relationships. In doing so you will be sure to minimize your disappointments.

I have two final points here. First, as personal relationships progress and become stronger, the parties involved enjoy doing things for each other. Their gestures express how they feel about each other. Those "doing things" are not a condition of the relationship but an extension of it. The attitude is "I do things to please you because I care for you, not because I want anything in return."

Second, a quick way of determining the quality of a personal-based relationship is to ask yourself, "On a scale of one to ten, how defensive do I have to be with this person?" You will find that the less defensive you feel in a relationship, the better its quality.

3. Be cautious when crossing the line from one type of relationship to another.

Can you cross the line from a marketing-based to a personal-based relationship or from a personal-based to a marketing-based relationship? That is, can you have both types of relationships with the same person? The answer is a conditional yes.

Crossing from a Marketing-Based to a Personal-Based Relationship

We have had a marketing-based relationship with our family physician for over twenty years. While we respect his medical knowledge and skills, we also were neighbors and enjoyed his and his wife's company. Wishing to develop a personal relationship with him, without jeopardizing our physician-patient relationship, we had to separate the two roles.

The way we successfully did it was to (1) not discuss our medical concerns when we were together socially, (2) pay our bills as we would to any professional whose services we employ, (3) expect no more than we would from any other professional, and (4) make our office visits "strictly business."

By not confusing our personal relationship with our marketing affiliation, we can enjoy both.

Realize that this transition evolves and cannot be forced. If, for example, you value someone's services, i.e., the things he or she does for you in exchange for payment, but you also are attracted to that person because of his or her personal qualities, you may indeed want to develop a personal relationship with that person. Assuming the feelings are mutual, when you begin this transitional process, do not use the personal relationship to gain advantage in the marketing association.

Jim, a manager with one of my client companies, ran into a problem with one of his subordinates who attempted to do just that. Their marketing-based affiliation, which blossomed into a personal one, seemed to be going fine until Wally (the subordinate) asked Jim for a favor—a special privilege he would not request under normal circumstances. Offended by Wally's attempt to take advantage of their friendship, Jim not only denied Wally the favor, but also ended their personal relationship. Wally, rightfully believing that his inappropriate behavior would hurt his future in this job, found a position elsewhere.

This consequence could have been avoided had Wally viewed the relationships with Jim as two separate ones: employee at work, friend away from work. By expecting more as an employee than the marketing contract called for, he also abused the friendship.

Again, if you want to cross the line successfully from a marketing-based to personal-based relationship, realize that they are distinct functions and should not be mixed.

Crossing from a Personal-Based to a Marketing-Based Relationship

Nowhere do you see greater difficulties in crossing the line than in family businesses where key people employ other family members and friends. Although there is nothing basically wrong with this practice, it can cause conflicts and morale problems if standards of performance and conduct are looser for relatives and friends than for everyone else. If you are a principal in a family-owned business, you can avoid potential difficulties with your regular employees and with the relatives and friends you employ by making sure they and the people supervising them are aware of the following conditions of their employment:

1. While we have a personal relationship outside of this environment, in this organization you are an employee.

2. As an employee, you are expected to abide by the same standards and rules as everyone else.

3. As an employee, your performance will be evaluated as objectively as everyone's is.

4. You are not to request special privileges just because we are relatives or friends.

5. Once you leave this place of business, our personal relationship may resume.

6. During our personal time, we will make every effort not discuss any business issues that involve you.

If you are a relative or friend employed in a family-owned business, you would be wise to follow the above rules even though they are not stated. Doing so will enable you to enjoy the benefits of both your marketing and personal relationships.

CHAPTER 2

Dealing with Life's Problems

Life's problems abound. To cope with and overcome them successfully, you need a solid foundation of principles to guide you and tools to activate them. Once the five principles discussed in this chapter become part of you, you will be better equipped to solve your problems and have additional wisdom for building on your foundation.

The principles discussed in this chapter are deceptively simple in the way they are stated. Don't be fooled by their simplicity and rush through them. Rather, take your time to learn each concept until you are comfortable enough to use it. Then move on to the next one.

The specific principles discussed in this chapter are

Express all problems in positive terms.
Make certain your wants are reasonable.
Solve problems by facing, not avoiding, them.
Think in shades of gray, not black and white.
Be cautious of extreme behaviors and attitudes.

4. Express all problems in positive terms.

If, by some magical means, you could wish away all your problems, would you? That's a tough question to answer, since your response depends on how you view and define a problem.

If you see problems as opportunities in work clothes, you certainly would not want to wish them away. Nor would you want to wish away problems you saw as challenges that could lead to a better life.

But if you consider problems to be pains, heavy burdens, difficulties, or major impediments created by other people or unfortunate conditions, you would probably welcome any means of making your problems vanish. Why? Because, viewed negatively, problems are enemies.

Just listen to how people with such views typically express their personal and interpersonal problems. "My problem is that I have an unreasonable boss." "My problem is that I can't seem to motivate my people." "My problem is that I'm going nowhere in this job." "My problem is that I've got too many things to do and not enough time to do them." "My problem is that I'm not organized; that's why I'm constantly tired." "My problem is that I'm burdened with problems." Those negatively stated problems make the persons expressing them feel like victims who are at the mercy of whoever or whatever is causing their discomfort.

Before we consider a more effective way of viewing and expressing problems, take a few minutes to write down your answer to this question: *At this stage of your life, what is your major work-related role?* Now, write down specifically all the things you do in this role, i.e., describe your major responsibilities. Let me share with you mine.

As a university professor, which is my major work-related role, my main responsibilities are to teach my students principles that will help them become more effective managers, to teach them how to think wisely about important work-related and personal problems, to make the courses I teach interesting, and to assess how well my students have grasped the material discussed in each course. Of course, under each of those responsibilities are a host of activities, such as answering questions, upgrading the material I present, and more.

Look at your list. Notice that the common thread running through all your activities is solving problems. That's what all of us get paid to do, regardless of our formal title, position, or occupation: we solve problems. Physicians solve medical problems, lawyers solve legal problems, managers solve administrative, production, and people-related problems, and parents solve household and family-related problems.

What makes something a problem? Simply put, *a problem is a discrepancy between what you want and what actually is.* And because the wants not being satisfied are *your* wants, these are *your* problems. If, for example, a client does not follow a plan I recommend, it is my problem. If a student resists my request to participate in class discussions, that is my problem. Or if my physician or lawyer isn't helping me resolve my concerns, that's also my problem. But I'm glad these are my problems. Because being their owner I can do something about them, just as you can about your problems.

To deal effectively with your problems, you first must define them in positive terms, terms that express precisely what *you* want or need. You won't deal with them effectively if you define them in terms of what you don't have, what others are not doing, what people are doing that prevent you from getting what you want, or what difficulties you're experiencing. Such statements do little more than upset you and deter you from solving your problems.

Let's compare the differences in sound between problems that are negatively stated and those expressed in positive terms. We'll use the ones we mentioned above.

"My problem is that I have an unreasonable boss."
"I need to discuss with my boss how he could help me be more effective." Or
"I need to let my boss know what I need from her so I can give her what she wants."

"My problem is that I can't seem to motivate my people."
"I have to determine from my people what I need to do to turn them on." Or
"I have to figure out what it takes to increase my people's productivity."

"My problem is that I'm going nowhere in this job."
"I want a job that makes greater use of my knowledge and skills and offers greater opportunities for advancement." Or
"I need to find a job that has greater growth potential."

"My problem is that I've got too many things to do and not enough time to do them."
"I need to figure out how to fulfill my job responsibilities in the time I have available."

"My problem is that I'm not organized; that's why I'm constantly tired."
"I have to find out why I'm constantly tired; maybe if I get organized it will help."

"My problem is that I'm burdened with problems."
"What can I do to unburden myself of the problems I have?"

When you express problems in positive terms you place yourself on a road that leads to solutions. Notice, none of the positively stated problems conveys a "poor me, I am a victim of my conditions" attitude. Nor do any of them sound like complaints. Rather, each statement *assumes* the discrepancy between what the person wants and what actually is, but it focuses on the action necessary to solve the problem. People who state problems negatively not only feel like victims, but they also get stuck in a feeling-sorry-for-themselves mode that can lead to unproductive anger, frustration, a feeling of helplessness, and even depression.

Although we will talk later about how to solve problems, for now practice expressing negatively stated problems in positive language.

Practice Instructions

Write down, *in positive terms,* your most pressing problems at home and at work. Next, for each one ask yourself, "Does this problem state specifically what I want that I'm not getting, a need I have to fulfill, or an action I have to take?" A "yes" to every problem statement is evidence that you successfully completed this assignment. Remember, *knowing specifically what you want is the first step to getting it.*

More Examples

I can't seem to do anything right.
I need to figure out what I have to do to correct this.

My problem is that I can't afford this.
I've got to find a way to purchase this product so it doesn't create financial burdens for me.

I get no respect from my boss.
I want my boss to tell me what I need to do to get respect from him.

Why aren't they promoting me?
I need to find out what it takes to make myself more promotable.

MAJOR PRINCIPLE TO GUIDE YOU: *Problems stated in positive terms lead to solutions; problems stated in negative terms lead to distress and feelings of helplessness. Always state problems in positive terms.*

5. Make certain your wants are reasonable.

Now that you've expressed your problems as specific wants, or in some other positive terms, you have to assess how reasonable those wants are. Doing so will prepare you for the next step, which is discussed under Principle 6 (solve problems by facing, not avoiding, them). Before we continue, however, let me say that there is a major distinction between a "want" and "it sure would be nice if _____" A want is potentially attainable, but "it sure would be nice if _____" is magical thinking.

The chance of attaining a want depends on how reasonable it is. For example, if you want a position that requires more education or experience than you possess, that want is not very reasonable since the chance of you being chosen over more qualified applicants is low. But this want would be highly reasonable if you had the qualifications, which then would increase your chances of obtaining the position.

To determine how reasonable a particular want is, first specify in writing, next to each want, the person who can conceivably help you fulfill it. (If you are the only person who can make your want happen, say so: "I and only I can fulfill this want.") Then, answer the following questions, using a scale of 1 (low) to 10 (high).

1. To what extent does this person desire to do what you want?

2. To what extent does this person have the intelligence, knowledge, skill, discipline, or power to accomplish this want? That is, to what extent is this person capable of fulfilling your want?

3. How much control or influence do you yourself have over all the forces that affect the fulfillment of this want?

Most people who have gone through this exercise with me discover two things. First, unless you have total control over *all* the forces that affect your wants, the reasonableness of those wants is less than 100 percent. Second, the only wants that potentially are *totally* reasonable are those that only you are willing and able to make happen. All your other wants vary in their degree of reasonableness.

For example, wanting to stay in decent shape (which is a positive version of "I'm too fat") is completely reasonable, assuming the desire and discipline are a "9" or "10," because the actions needed to accomplish that want are within your control. However, if your reason for staying in shape is that you want to be a model or a star tennis player, both those wants are less than totally reasonable, since forces you do not control must inevitably become involved.

Here's another example. Suppose you want a 10-percent salary increase and, based on your excellent work performance, you deserve it. That want is not very reasonable if the company's salary cap is 5 percent. A more reasonable want would be stated as follows: "I want to do everything in my power to demonstrate my value to the company and to show them that I'm worthy of the highest raise they will allow."

If obtaining the results you want is not fully within your control, the questions you must ask yourself are: "What can I do to increase my chances of getting what I want? How can I gain the cooperation of the person or people who can help me achieve that want?"

Many years ago, when I started teaching, I had a strong desire to be liked by *all* my students. Of course, I wasn't. But I was too naïve to realize that my upsets and disappointments resulted from an unreasonable want. When I became aware that being liked by my students is out of my control, and that I was setting myself up for disappointments, I changed my desire. I told myself, "I want to be the very best teacher I can be; I want to stimulate my students to think." Those reasonable wants not only ended my disappointments, but they also created exciting challenges, which resulted in satisfying successes.

Recently, during a class discussion on this subject, a student asked me, "Is it reasonable to want my boss to politely *ask* me to do things, rather than ordering me to do them?"

"Of course it's reasonable," I said. "But *how* reasonable depends on his inclination and desire to change. So, let me ask you, how does he talk to the other people in the office?"

"When he talks to managers or customers he's very polite. He sounds like a different person. But when he talks to me or to other clerical help he's abrupt and demanding."

"Obviously, he knows how to be cordial, but to increase your chances of him behaving that way toward the clerical staff you have to restate your want," I said.

After a few attempts, Melissa stated her want as follows: "I want Mr. Holmes to be aware of how he comes across to the clerical people; I also want him to know that we would be more productive if he *asked* us to do things rather than demanded we do them."

The following week Melissa informed the class that she expressed her concerns to her boss and made her desires known. She also told the class that until she spoke to him about this issue he was unaware of his behavior, and thanked her for bringing it to his attention. Since then, according to Melissa, his demeanor toward all personnel has been more respectful.

If, after putting your wants through the three-question "reasonable test," you discover a want that fails the test, rewrite it and make the want more attainable. During this rewriting phase keep in mind an old Indian proverb, "He who looks for what cannot be obtained will endure much trouble."

6. Solve problems by facing, not avoiding, them.

When you have a problem, how do you *typically* deal with it? Do you find someone to blame, make excuses, attack the source of the problem, sulk, hold grudges, deny its existence, minimize its importance, exaggerate its difficulty, disparage yourself, or react in other ways that don't help you solve the problem? Or do you view your problem as a challenge that tests your mettle, see it as an opportunity to obtain something you currently lack, consider all possible options for solving it, and then take appropriate steps that lead you to a reasonable solution?

The Defensive Strategy

"Defenders" *characteristically* approach problems the first way. They are like turtles, who, in the face of actual or potential danger, retract into their shells and wait until the threat disappears.

All a turtle can do is wait, since he cannot move forward when his head and limbs are inside his shell.

People, being smarter and more creative than turtles, have many more defenses to protect them from ego-threatening and other fear-producing conditions. Understandably, because defenses are like emotional clothing, all of us employ them to a reasonable degree, particularly when the danger is real. For defenders, however, self-protection is an automatic, primary reaction to the fear their problems trigger. Because defenders tend to see the world as threatening and people as adversaries, their self-protective guard is always up, dictating how they deal with difficulties. As one defender I know told me, "When things are not going the way I'd like, my baser instincts unconsciously come into play. It's like a nerve is touched. When that happens, I react in ways I am most accustomed to. I lash out at those who are dearest to me; sometimes I take out my anger on myself."

Regardless of what form unconscious defensiveness takes, whether it's lashing out at others, getting uncontrollably angry at oneself, pointing fingers, being dishonest with others and oneself, procrastinating, or acting irresponsibly and then justifying those actions, the result is the same: no forward movement, no solving of problems. Realize that *any attitude or behavior that does not move you one step closer to what you really want is defensive.*

"But," you say, "suppose what I really want is to protect myself from the threat of negative consequences. Doesn't my defensiveness give me what I want?" Of course it does. That's why I make a distinction between unconscious and conscious defensiveness. Defenders are *unconsciously defensive* and, therefore, they don't realize that their reactions are emotional and non-rational. After all, it is their natural way of dealing with problems. When you are consciously defensive, however, you *choose* to protect yourself and that's OK much of the time.

The following are examples of *consciously* defensive statements:

"To avoid getting a traffic ticket, I drive cautiously and am careful not to exceed the speed limit."

"If I know from past experience that talking to my friend about his weight problem will upset him, I avoid the topic."

"When my boss asks for my opinion about a decision he's made, I agree with him because if I don't he questions my judgment until I approve."

"I refuse to ask John for a favor because I don't want to be rejected another time."

Those actions are rational and stem from knowledge and experience. They are learned behaviors, like when children stay clear of hot stoves after some painful experiences or know not to say things that they've learned are "no-nos." Such avoidance reactions are the children's conscious defenses against getting hurt or being admonished by their parents.

Conscious defensiveness is perfectly reasonable, as long as it is not excessive. But, like unconscious defensiveness, it is a protective action whose main function is to prevent the negative consequences you anticipate.

If you believe yourself to be *characteristically* defensive, you would be wise to reduce that tendency, since not doing so will stifle your development—either personal, professional, or both. You can take initial steps to reduce your unconscious defensiveness by being aware when others are defensive. When you spot it, ask yourself, "Will that reaction enable this person to move one step closer to what he wants?" "Will that reaction enable this person to solve his problem?" Once you increase your sensitivity to other people's defensiveness and see how unproductive it is, you'll be able to see it in yourself, reduce its frequency, and replace it with a more effective approach.

Since a problem-solving strategy is the only effective means of propelling you toward the things you want most, let's discuss the elements of that approach.

The Problem-Solving Strategy

To solve any "people problem," you need to (1) know *specifically* what you want, (2) make sure what you want is reasonable, and (3) have a plan of action for fulfilling each reasonable want. Since you already know how to state your problem in positive terms and know how to determine if what you want is reasonable, let's build on that knowledge to help you solve problems rationally. You will gain the most value from this process by choosing one current pressing problem and following the procedure outlined in the "Problem-Solving Work Sheet."

Problem-Solving Work Sheet

BACKGROUND

Statement of Problem: State your problem in terms of what you want that you are not now getting. Remember, be specific and concrete. Another way of formulating the problem is to answer the question "How could this person [whether it's you, if you are the source of the problem, or someone else] satisfy my desire?"

Symptoms of Problem: How is this problem exhibited? What, specifically, is this person doing or not doing that's creating your problem?

When Did These Symptoms Begin? Consider a time-line, beginning with your first contact with the person and ending with the present. Pinpoint when you first became aware of the symptoms. If possible, specify an exact date.

What Conditions or Events Could Have Triggered the Symptoms? Answer this question only if the symptoms began to surface some time other than the beginning of the time-line.

What Have You Done to Correct the Problem? State, specifically, what you've said or done.

What Have Been the Results of Your Efforts? What did the person say or do? What symptoms still persist?

What Else Do You Need to Know to Help You Understand the Nature and Possible Causes of Your Problem? This question is simply another attempt to help you consider things you may have overlooked.

ACTION PLAN

Meet privately with the person who is the source of your problem. State your problem (you may begin with "I've got a problem"), its symptoms, the effect those symptoms have on you or others, and what, specifically, you want from this person.

Ask the person if what you want is reasonable.

Assuming it is reasonable, ask the person how the two of you can resolve the problem—that is, what has to be done to eliminate the symptoms and prevent them from recurring.

Ask how you can ensure that your agreements will be honored and, if they are inadvertently breached, how you can gently inform him or her.

If the person deems your want unreasonable, discuss it until you can agree.

In short, "What *specifically* do I want?" and "What *exactly* must I do to get it?" are the two most important questions you can ask yourself when faced with a problem.

A variation of the "want question" also works when you feel the urge to be harsh and when you sense your emotions going out of control. When those negative feelings come over you, *stop.* Say nothing and do nothing. Instead, ask yourself, "If I give in to my impulse, will it get me what I *really* want?" Your negative response to this rational question will jar loose your intellect from the tight grip of your emotions and redirect you toward a reasonable problem-solving route. Another approach that may work for you, as it has for me, when you feel like saying something that could come back to haunt you, is to ask yourself, "What's the point? What will I gain by saying it?"

Reinforcing the Problem-Solving Strategy

If you are like many people, your *natural* inclination is to be defensive. However, that doesn't mean you have to yield to that tendency. Assuming you have taken the initial step to reduce your unconscious defensiveness by being aware of it in others, and assuming you have begun to employ the problem-solving strategy outlined above, you are already making strides to reduce your defensive tendencies. But you can reduce such reactions even more by intensifying your conscious effort.

Conscious effort is what alcoholics—who are naturally addicted to liquor—put forth when they join Alcoholics Anonymous. That's what overeaters—who are naturally addicted to food—put forth when they go on a food- and calorie-reduction program. That's what average athletes put forth when they work extra hard to compete with gifted athletes.

In each of those instances, giving in to natural inclinations is easy. It is also evidence of weakness. Is being defensive *your* natural tendency? If it is, you can begin to win the fight by *consciously* making an effort to change. The two approaches I will suggest are similar to those used to replace bad habits with good ones.

First, make a sign of the thing you want to remember and hang it someplace where you can see it every day—perhaps on top of your bathroom mirror. Duplicate the sign on a three-by-five-inch index card and keep it with you at all times; read it several times a day until the rule or principle comes naturally to you.

Begin with this sign: *WHAT SPECIFICALLY DO I WANT? HOW CAN I GET IT?* These questions will serve as constant reminders of what things are most important to you in any given situation. Eventually, this rational approach to dealing with problems will replace whatever negative, defensive forces prevent you from moving forward.

Second, before responding to anyone whose words or behaviors trigger an emotional reaction, say nothing for five seconds—nothing. Then, when your brain is functioning and your emotions are under control, respond. You can speed up the development of this positive habit by making another sign (and duplicating it on a three-by-five-inch index card) that reads: *T H I N K: SAY NOTHING FOR FIVE SECONDS.*

If you conscientiously practice those two methods of dealing with problems, you will be amazed at how quickly you can replace a self-defeating habit with a productive one.

I used the exact same approach many years ago to overcome my self-defeating habit of procrastinating. The signs read: *DO IT NOW.* I hung them in my office and bathroom, and kept a three-by-five-inch duplicate in my wallet. Whenever the thought of procrastinating entered my brain, I saw the sign and right then did whatever I was supposed to do. It took me six months to break the habit.

When Others Are Defensive

OK, so you promise yourself to reduce your defensiveness and become more of a problem solver. That's great. But, since others don't have your newfound knowledge and wisdom, you have to deal with defensiveness when you confront someone with a problem. Here is how to do it. Accept that person's defense, since that's his reality, and ease him back to the issue at hand. Realize that your objective is to resolve the problem; getting caught up in a defensive-offensive dialogue only delays its resolution. Consider the following two examples:

SARAH: When will the project I gave you be finished?

JOSEPH: I've been too busy to get it done when I said I would.

SARAH: I realize you've been busy. But I need to have that project completed by Wednesday. What help do you need to make that deadline?

By accepting his defense and focusing on her main concern, Sarah defuses Joseph's initial need to protect himself and gets him thinking about how to solve her problem. Had Sarah lashed out at Joseph, he would have gotten even more defensive.

> MICHAEL: If your explanation had been better I wouldn't have made those mistakes.
>
> ENID: That's probably true. But now that you realize what has to be done, would you please make the corrections?

Your acceptance of a defense need not be elaborate, nor do you have to remember specific words. You could, for example, show your acceptance by being silent for a moment or two, just long enough to give you time to think before you deal with the issue that concerns you. You could also simply say, "OK," and then bring the defender back to the issue. In short, all you have to remember when faced with a defensive verbal reaction are three rules:

1. Accept people's defensiveness, since they are entitled to protect themselves. Acceptance says, in effect, "You are entitled to believe whatever you like."

2. Never tell defenders not to be defensive or say, "You're being defensive." Such statements strip them of their emotional clothing and intensifies their defensiveness. Also, telling them not to be defensive or chastising them for it is certain to create dissension.

3. After accepting the defense, bring the discussion back to the issue, i.e., the essence of your problem.

7. Think in Shades of Gray, Not Black and White.

"People are either good or bad, right or wrong." "If I can't be the best at something, I usually don't attempt it, or I quit early

in the going." "If it's not my way, it's no way." "Unless it's perfect, it's no good." "I don't need anyone's help; I can do everything myself." Those are emotionally based, defensive
statements that make no sense. Furthermore, people whose
actions are influenced by such extreme beliefs miss out on
many opportunities and set themselves up for major disappointments.

Do the above statements reflect your views? If they do, and
you're tired of the often negative consequences of such
extreme attitudes, welcome to the beautiful world of rational
gray—a world where both emotions and intelligence are tempered with good judgment, and where good judgment, not
black/white thinking, is rewarded.

You will significantly reduce your disappointments and benefit in countless other ways by practicing the points and tools
discussed in this section. Since many of our disappointments
come from people whose services we employ, we'll begin by
considering how to gain maximum value from professional
people we must deal with.

Grading Professional Competence

To start living in the world of rational gray, you must develop
criteria for judging professional competence. Why? Because all
professionals in their respective fields bear the same occupational title, although their individual abilities vary. Regardless
of whether they are excellent, mediocre, or incompetent, all
doctors are "doctors," all lawyers are "lawyers," all plumbers are
"plumbers," all teachers are "teachers," etc. As a consumer of
professional services, you will have to cast aside your image and
prejudgment of people's occupational titles, and judge professionals on reasonable criteria. Here is one way to do it.

Using the 1-10 continuum we've used before (with 1 being
low and 10 being high), you can rate the quality of practition-
ers you deal with in every occupational group. Then, depending upon how well they meet your criteria, you can decide, with
greater objectivity, whether you want to do business with them.

While you may not be able to judge their technical competence, their demeanor says a great deal about them and could serve as a reasonable basis for your judgment. For example, to have me as a client, people whose services I employ *at least* have to return my phone calls, be on time for appointments, be reasonably civil toward me and anyone working for them, honor their promises to me, answer my questions, and respect my views on the problems that bring me to them. In short, I have to feel they care enough about me and my problems to listen to me and to extend to me the common courtesies everyone deserves. Depending on the professional and how confident I feel about his or her abilities, I may or may not check references.

Automatic turn-offs for me, in addition to a person's failure to meet my minimum requirements, are alarmist reactions, outlandish claims or promises, extreme solutions, tendencies toward defensiveness, and any actions or reactions that cause me seriously to question the person's technical competence, human qualities, and wisdom. I am particularly leery when someone's response to one of my questions is "Don't worry; you can trust me." Or "I can't explain it to you because you wouldn't understand."

In short, when I deal with professionals, I want to feel they are logical and in control. I want to be totally confident that I am in good hands, and the services I contract for will be delivered and will be the quality I anticipate. And I want the respect I, as a paying customer or client, deserve. Don't you?

Another Application of the "Continuum Tool"

People often talk in extreme and nonspecific language. Some examples: "Sheila is insensitive." "Gary is overly sensitive." "You didn't do as good a job as I would have liked." "My boss is unfair." "You did a good job." "Howard is inconsiderate." "We have an OK relationship." "Your attitude needs to improve."

Had you made any of those statements, you would probably know what you were referring to, but the people to whom you'd be talking would not. Why? One reason is that abstract words and labels have different meanings to each of us. For example, recently a student told me that his boss was fair. I asked, "Fair in what way?"

He said, "She treats everybody the same."

"But everybody has different needs and, therefore, requires different amounts of attention and kinds of treatment," I said. "If she treats everyone the same, isn't she being unfair?"

Continuing our discussion of what constitutes fairness, we agreed that fairness takes into account individual differences. This productive talk would not have occurred had I simply accepted his original statement.

Not only do abstract terms vary in meaning, but also in degree. There are, for example, different degrees of insensitivity, sensitivity, inconsiderateness, unfairness, quality, and just about any characteristic. But those differences—the shades of gray—are lost in such words' vagueness. For example, in the statement "Sheila is insensitive," the speaker gives the impression that Sheila lacks sensitivity toward everyone she deals with, when actually she may have only committed one insensitive act. Similarly, in the statement "Howard is inconsiderate," Howard may have committed one or two inconsiderate acts, but that does not warrant the label "inconsiderate."

To avoid misunderstandings caused by abstract and extreme terms, be precise and use examples. Consider the differences in the following statements:

"My boss is so insensitive."
"When I told my boss about the problems I was having at home, he said, 'Will those problems interfere with the project you're working on?' He didn't even ask me what those problems were or if I wanted to talk about them."

"John's attitude is terrible."
"John badmouths his boss, constantly complains about the demands of his job, and comes in ten minutes late four out of five days a week."

Admittedly, it is more difficult to be specific and give examples. But think of it as a way of preventing misunderstandings and the negative consequences they cause.

Another way of preventing consequences of misunderstandings is to avoid generalizations such as "always" and "never" when you mean sometimes or rarely. Just recently, sitting in a restaurant, I overheard the people next to me having a loud, heated argument. "You *always* get defensive," one of them said.

Well, you and I know that's not true. The accuser may have felt that way, or he may have wanted to make a stronger case with his generalization. But all it did was cause the conversation to deteriorate into a variation of a "No, I'm not," "Yes, you are" dialogue that seemed to go nowhere. They finally got up, seemingly angry at each other, and left without finishing their meal.

Once you get into the habit of being specific and using examples to make your point, you will request others to do the same. Rather than risk misunderstanding people, you will ask for clarification before you respond. You might ask, "How do you know Lynn is angry?" "What did Gary say or do that makes you think he's *overly* sensitive?" "On a scale of one to ten, how good was it?" "What would make the job better?" "What do you mean by OK?" "What exactly is wrong with my attitude?" And, with regard to generalizations, you might ask, "Always?" "Never?" "What do you mean, *always?*" "Do you really mean *never?*"

By training yourself to view generalizations as shades of gray, you will not only come up with questions that help you better understand what people are talking about, but you will be less tempted to think in terms of black/white and all/nothing.

Evidence that Gray Is Sensible, and How to Develop Gray Thinking

You and I would certainly feel more secure if we could confidently place people and events into clearly defined and neatly labeled boxes such as positive or negative, good or bad, and right or wrong. Then we wouldn't have to think, contemplate options, or rely on our judgment when faced with important decisions. But consider the price. Rigid people are blinded to much of what's before them. They see only things they want to see, not what actually is. By failing to see beyond the obvious and past their narrow perspectives, they miss out on excellent opportunities—those that knock subtly—and potentially fruitful relationships.

That is not the case with Bill, the operations manager of a family-owned business. As evidence of his gray thinking, he shared with me his philosophy about the seminars he frequently attends. "When I go to a seminar I feel if I get just one idea, one thought, one method that can have a positive effect on my life, it's a good seminar, and whatever time and money I spend is a good investment. I can honestly say I have never been to a bad seminar, although some were better than others."

This same person looks for gold in any form and in every experience, regardless of how something appears on the surface. As you might predict, he gets more from life than people whose actions and reactions are dictated by superficial appearances.

Realize this: if your stereotypical or superficial view of someone or something is negative, you may be focusing on the *hole* rather than the *whole*. You're seeing only what is not, and not seeing what is. By bemoaning what is not and failing to acknowledge what is, you lose out on the benefits that the whole can provide. That would be like deciding not to buy doughnuts because they lack solid centers.

People who see the *whole* of course acknowledge what isn't and other negative characteristics of the whole, but they also see the positive elements that may be present. They are sufficiently flexible and reasonable to consider both positive and negative characteristics of a person or an experience.

If your tendency is to make negative judgments about someone or something because you are displeased with parts of it, consider bringing a *W* into your life. You'll be glad you did. You will get more from life if you don't allow yourself to be fooled by glitter alone (in whatever form it appears) and if you are not disillusioned by superficial negative appearances. Superficial appearances, good or bad, are not accurate indicators of what actually constitutes the *whole*.

You can learn to be a gray, flexible thinker, but it requires considerable effort. The following thoughts and points, which I urge you to think about, will guide you:

Bending, when appropriate, i.e., when warranted by evidence or conditions, is a strength, not a weakness. It reflects thoughtful, reasonable thinking. It acknowledges the indisputable fact that there is a large range of grays between black and white.

Since the superficial represents a small fraction of the whole, look beyond and beneath the surface. You may find gold, opportunities, and challenges that only become apparent if you search and dig for them.

Consider what's possible rather than dwell on the impossible or improbable; focus on what is rather than what is not.

Accept the fact that nobody and nothing is absolutely perfect. By doing so you will not get needlessly upset when people fall short of perfection.

Realize there are no magical solutions to complex problems. To solve them requires effort, perseverance, and determination.

Since taking risks is essential to personal success, take reasonable risks that offer you a good chance of winning, but, if success does not materialize, that's OK. At least you tried.

Trust your judgment. While you may be wrong, at least your decisions will stem from reason rather than emotion.

Finally, realize that even a good quality carried to the extreme has negative consequences. For proof, consider the extremes of caring, loving, friendliness, and carefulness. They become smothering, possessiveness, familiarity, and fear.

If you want further confirmation that gray thinking is sensible and is a major characteristic of wise managers, consider the next principle, which highlights the negative consequences of extreme behaviors and attitudes. Also, it talks about why people who exhibit them should be dealt with cautiously.

8. Be Cautious of Extreme Behaviors and Attitudes.

To appreciate fully the beauty of rational gray thinking, you need to see the dangers of black/white, extreme thinking, which is essentially a defensive reaction that *may* produce short-term benefits, but definitely sabotages long-term objectives. Your awareness of how extreme attitudes and behaviors can harm you will both reinforce your resolve to "think gray" and improve your ability to deal with people who exhibit a black/white mentality.

Extremists, by definition, fall into two categories: the *low end* of both the *flexibility continuum* and the *sensitivity-toward-others continuum*, and the *high end* of these two continua. Let's consider how each type views the world and how they function.

Low-End Extremists

These, you recall from Principle 7, are rigid people whose actions and decisions mainly stem from emotions, which are nonrational. Jim, whose motto could easily be "I've got my mind made up; don't confuse me with facts or logic," typifies such individuals. His reactions are knee jerk, indiscriminate, and predictable. Lacking confidence in his judgment, he finds it easier to place people into positive or negative boxes. If he views you as a friend, one who shares his beliefs, you can do no wrong. After all, since you are like him you must be all right. Therefore, even if one of your actions were seen by most people as thoughtless and inappropriate, he would defend you.

However, if you are one of those unfortunates who are in his negative box, you can do nothing right. Even if your actions were viewed favorably by most people, Jim would find some fault with them so he could justify his negative attitude toward you. No evidence or logic would alter his stance. Why? Because his decisions are predetermined by his rigidity. And so, people tend to remain in his negative or positive boxes for life.

Since he maintains the position that things not done his way must be wrong, he always fights to do things his way. Yes, he is also a racial and religious bigot. And he is meticulous to a fault because everything has its place, just like people.

Rigid people tend to make statements that leave no room for exceptions, such as: "It's my policy and I *never* deviate from it." "I don't *ever* give suggestions because if people follow them and they don't work out they'll blame me." "I don't want you *ever* to say anything bad about _____ [a person in a positive box]." "*All* [women, men, or whatever] are the same." In short, they talk in absolute, not relative, terms. And because they do, they miss out on the positive characteristics in what they label as "bad" and fail to see the negatives in what they label as "good."

Concerning their sensitivity toward others, low-end extremists are like smoke detectors with faulty batteries. Oblivious to the pain their abrasive, abusive, and inconsiderate comments and actions cause people they supposedly care about, they keep doing it, insisting that their actions are not wrong or that the people they hurt are "overly sensitive." To them, their behavior seems perfectly normal.

People on the extreme low end of the sensitivity-toward-others continuum pay a high price for their malfunctioning people-sensor. While some may get away with it for a time, and may even be financially successful, they are the exception, not the rule. Most people do pay a heavy price for their lack of sensitivity. The prices to such business owners and managers include loss of valued personnel, loss of customers, poor performance from employees, low morale, missed opportunities, and ultimately a decline in profits or worse.

In their personal lives, the price is even heavier, both emotionally and financially, as one of my acquaintances discovered. Marv, who thought his relationship with his wife was just fine, learned how wrong he was when she woke him in the middle of the night to tell him she had had enough and wanted to end their twenty-five-year marriage. At first, he couldn't believe what he heard. But when he realized she was serious, he said, "I wasn't aware you were unhappy. Why didn't you tell me?" She replied, "I've been telling you for the past five years, but obviously my complaints didn't register with you. Now it's too late."

After telling me this, he admitted, "I really wasn't aware. I thought everything was going well." Actually, it only appeared fine to him because he failed to recognize the symptoms that ultimately resulted in a painful divorce. He thought, for example, that it was normal for his wife to complain about him working too much ("Don't all wives?"). He also thought nothing of his wife's complaints that they don't do things together, that he doesn't call when he's going to be late for dinner, that he rarely has time for the children, and that she doesn't feel appreciated or loved. He didn't think those complaints were unusual. So what made him think everything was fine? Tangible evidence. They had a nice house, in an attractive suburban community, and his wife and children did not want for anything money could buy. As far as Marv was concerned, he was doing his part to make a good life for his family.

High-End Extremists

These people's extreme flexibility also stems from their lack of confidence in their judgment. Distrusting their decision-making ability, they allow themselves to be pushed and pulled in all directions. They'll go along with anyone they believe in and, like chameleons, will change to blend with their environment, whether or not the change makes sense. Fearing that they will be disliked unless they give in to everyone's desires, their typical responses are: "I don't care; I'll go along with what everyone wants." "Whatever you say is OK with me." "I don't want to make waves."

Their extreme sensitivity toward others, like their extreme flexibility, not only stems from their overwhelming need to be liked, but also an inordinate fear of hurting others' feelings, intense fear of being rejected, and distorted perception of what's expected of them. Those needs and beliefs explain in part why such people have difficulty saying no and agree to any requests, regardless of the difficulties that may cause.

Millie, a customer representative who is known at the company she works for as "Mother Hen," personifies most high-end extremists I have known. Her "sensor" is typically activated by a frown, a failure of someone to greet her, or any out-of-the-ordinary action. While those actions may have no deep underlying meaning, Millie almost always misinterprets them. She may ask, "Are you upset?" "Is everything all right?" And, if you assure her there is nothing wrong, she will insist, "I know something is bothering you, but you're not telling me." "Did I do something to upset you?"

Her oversensitivity and overconcern gets to be annoying. Why? Because people don't like others to hover over them; they don't like to feel that their actions are being closely scrutinized; they don't like to feel that they have to watch everything they say and do. While Millie believes her sensitivity is helpful to other people, the fact that it is taken to the extreme makes it not helpful, although it makes her feel good to extend herself to others.

How to Deal with Extremists

While it is difficult to deal with highly emotional people, knowing that their reactions are defensive gives you an edge. Just employ the tool discussed under Principle 6: accept their defense and bring the discussion back to the issue. You might want to reread the section called "When Others Are Defensive" for examples. Consider also the following additional examples in dealing with both low-end and high-end extremists:

> "I know you feel strongly about your point of view, but I'd like,
> just for a moment, to consider my thoughts on the issue."

"Maybe you were preoccupied with other matters when I talked with you about this before, so let me reiterate my concerns."

"I appreciate your sensitivity, but let me assure you if something is wrong I'll tell you."

"I know you want to do the right thing, but let me tell you what I really need from you."

"I know you care about me, but I'd appreciate you trusting me enough to tell you when I need your help."

"May I ask you to put yourself in my shoes just for a moment? How would you deal with the issue if you were me?"

In Summary

Emotion tempered with reason is good. It's like spice that's added to quality food to enhance its taste. But when emotions alone dictate actions, as is the case with extreme behaviors, the results are about as unsavory as a spice-dominated dish.

Before you go on to the next chapter, think seriously about the following three points:

1. When emotions are in control, the brain is out of control. Since extreme behaviors and attitudes are generated and controlled by emotions, be careful of people so inclined.

2. Reduce your own extreme attitudes and behaviors, since, aside from the above reason, they are based on such faulty assumptions as "more is better," "holding fast to a point of view, regardless of evidence, is a sign of strength," and "the bottom line [financial reward] is all that matters."

3. Make important decisions when you are rational and delay making them when you are emotional.

CHAPTER 3

Developing a Sound Relationship with Yourself

A question frequently asked of me is "What is the most common cause of conflicts between people?" Although valued relationships are too complex to attribute conflicts to a single cause, to me, one stands out as being critical. Relationships most at risk are those in which people take each other for granted.

When you take someone for granted, your actions say, in effect, "Since there is no chance of losing you, because you belong to me, I don't have to think about you, nor do I have to be concerned with my behavior toward you. And because there is no danger of losing you, I don't have to be all that sensitive to you or responsive to your needs."

You, of course, know what would happen if you exhibited this attitude toward your customers, clients, or any other person whose relationship you want to preserve or cultivate. Chances are, their reactions would be no different than yours if *you* were taken for granted by people whose relationship you value.

Although few would dispute that all people like to feel special and, therefore, react poorly when taken for granted, it's puzzling why many people take *themselves* for granted. Such people view each day as no different from the next. They don't think about what they can do to make each day special. They don't think about who they are, what they want, what they've got going for them, and what they can do to vitalize their lives. Many don't even think about their physical health and what they must do to ensure better and longer lives. And because they don't think in terms of how they can be more effective managers of their own lives, they allow themselves to become victims of self-defeating attitudes and behaviors.

A wise manager, on the other hand, does not take himself for granted. Rather, he cares enough about himself to develop a healthy emotional and intellectual relationship with the most important person in his life. And because he has a good relationship with himself, he tends to be less defensive with others.

The principles and tools contained in this chapter will help you to respect and like yourself more. They will help you discover who you are as a person and the qualities that make you unique. They will provide you with principles and tools to help you maintain balance, and to be good to yourself. They will also help you replace self-defeating attitudes and behaviors with those that will activate your potential. By improving your relationship with yourself, you will pave the way to developing sound relationships with other people who matter to you both in your personal and professional life.

The principles discussed in this chapter are

Discover your strengths and empower yourself to use them.

Beware when false pride dictates your actions; replace it with genuine pride.

Focus on being and doing your best, not on pleasing others.

Avoid the "nice guy" trap; be forthright with yourself and others.

Reduce your excessive dependencies.

Concerning each thing you must do, tell yourself, "I *want* to do it," rather than, "I *should* do it."

To overpower your fear of failure, take one step at a time; reward yourself for each successful step you take.

Make specific and reasonable promises to yourself each day; fulfill those promises.

View the completion of each step toward a long-range goal as a fruit of your labor.

Set your standards reasonably high and live by them.

9. Discover your strengths and empower yourself to use them.

Bella, the mother of a friend of mine, constantly complained about her aches and pains. Some were undoubtedly real, but most were self-created due to a chronic negative attitude that she nurtured with her complaints about everything and everybody. Whenever anyone asked, "How are you, Bella?" she described in graphic detail what was wrong with her. She complemented her vivid descriptions of her physical condition with her whining commentary on life's difficulties, problems, and unfair treatment of her in particular. She usually ended her descriptions of her plight with "Why me?"—as if it were the final punctuation of her diatribe. If her sickly voice didn't convince you of her state, her gaunt and pale face did.

Her daughter, Judith, made numerous attempts to help Bella discover a world outside of herself. The words varied, but the pleas were the same: "Mom, why don't you go out and do things? Join a group, volunteer your services to a hospital, do something—anything but sit around complaining about how bad things are. You're making yourself sick."

Bella's retorts were predictably variations of the same theme.

"You don't understand; I'm sick. You think I enjoy being an invalid? You think I want to be a burden to you?" Exasperated, Judith would walk away. A few days later she'd try again, getting the same results as in her previous attempts. The only things that changed were Judith's ways of expressing her impatience and Bella's methods of resistance.

Their "I want to help you" versus "Leave me alone" exchanges went on for years. Frustrated by her efforts, Judith finally quit trying and accepted the fact that she had no choice but to tolerate her mother's narrow view of her abilities, which centered on her role as a housewife. But for Bella those abilities were a source of pride. She liked keeping a spotless house and cooking for her family and friends of her family. She also enjoyed sewing. After Judith had her first child, a little girl named Leah, Bella wanted to show her grandmotherly love in a special way. She wanted to do more than just baby-sit. So she started to make dresses. They were beautiful by anyone's standard, and varied in style from simple ones to two- and three-piece outfits.

Judith knew of her mother's sewing talent, but never appreciated the extent of her abilities. Bella also took her abilities for granted, and did not consider them extraordinary. She believed sewing was, along with cooking and cleaning, one of the requirements of a housewife.

Bella's creations were not unnoticed by people outside the family. "Where did you get that gorgeous outfit?" Judith's friends asked.

"My mother made it," she'd say with pride.

"What would she charge to make a dress for my daughter?" they'd ask.

"My mother only makes dresses for Leah. She used to make them for me when I was small. That's it. She won't do it for anyone else." That's what she told all the people who inquired about Bella's availability to outsiders.

One day after such an inquiry, Judith got a brainstorm: Why can't her mother market her services? Why *can't* she make dresses for others?

That night, determined to triumph over her mother's resistance to expand her horizons, Judith visited Bella. After the usual exchange of "How are you feeling?" "You know how I'm feeling; I'm sick," Judith said, "Listen, Mom, people keep asking me if you'll make outfits for their children like you make for Leah. And I tell them that you don't do it for anyone else. Still, they ask if you'll make an exception, and I tell them you won't. But I've been thinking. Do you really enjoy sewing?"

"You know I do," responded Bella.

"How about if I put an ad for you in the neighborhood newspaper? The ad would say you're a seamstress and available to fix dresses and make new dresses."

"I'm not good enough to do it for others," Bella said. "Besides, anybody can do what I do. Why should they pay me to do something they can do for themselves?"

Undaunted by her mother's resistance, Judith persisted. "What's the worst thing that can happen, Mom? Let me put the ad in and see if anyone is interested. You've got nothing to lose."

Worn down by Judith's perseverance, Bella said, "I'll think about it." The next morning, excited by her idea, Judith phoned Bella for her decision. Bella whined, "OK, go ahead and do it."

On the day the ad appeared, Bella received three calls from women who wanted their dresses altered. She made the appointments for the following day, when she received five more calls for a similar service.

That one ad brought Bella a large enough customer base to keep her profitably occupied for as many hours as she wanted to work. About six months later, the nature of her business changed. She almost completely gave up doing alterations, opting for the more profitable business of making new dresses. Her dressmaking business grew out of a request from one of her steady customers who was so thrilled with Bella's products that she spread the word.

One day I asked Judith about Bella's health. She smiled. "It's funny you ask," Judith said. "First of all, ever since my mother began this venture, she hasn't been sick. Second, I stopped inquiring about her health because the last couple times I asked how she felt she seemed annoyed. Once she said, 'I don't have time to think about it.' Another time she said, 'I'm too busy to be sick.' One more thing; I haven't heard her whine in a long time. She even talks like a confident businesswoman."

Bella continued to enjoy her profitable business and improved health for ten years after discovering her talent and empowering herself to use it. Her and her husband's desire for a more moderate climate prompted them to move from Chicago to California, where she developed a new dressmaking business, but on a smaller scale. According to Judith, Bella's health continued to be good until she died of natural causes.

How You Can Discover Your Strengths and Empower Yourself to Use Them

You, of course, know the classic story of Dorothy from Kansas and her friends: the brainless Scarecrow, the heartless Tinman, and the courageless Lion. It's an ageless story that reminds us of the abilities and powers we can find within ourselves if we only look.

The Scarecrow, the Tinman, the Lion, and Bella had one thing in common before they were convinced of their abilities: they took themselves for granted. They failed to see their virtues. They didn't realize that without the abilities they actually possessed, they could not have achieved what they did. Nor did they see their achievements as anything special.

If you tend to take yourself for granted and undervalue your abilities, it's time to stop and become aware of all the qualities and powers you possess. It's time to become your own Wizard. Here's how.

This project may require (although it's not necessary) the help of one other person you respect and trust fully. The person, if you want to go this route, needs to be someone who cares deeply about you—deeply enough to be totally honest with you. Keep that person in mind, since you will need his or her help later. For now, locate a quiet place that has a table to write on and bring to the table your notebook, the one I suggested earlier that you purchase, and a pen.

STEP ONE

Imagine looking in a full length mirror. Then, when you see yourself clearly, write the words *I see a person who* at the top of the first page. Next, complete the sentence in as many *positive* descriptive phrases that come to mind, using one line for each response. Consider *every* characteristic and skill you see that's positive. Include both physical and personal qualities, and *every* skill you can think of; don't be shy. Two cautions: (1) Do not use single words to complete the sentences and (2) do not rush this project or any parts of it; it may require several sittings.

Consider the following examples:

—is gray haired and distinguished looking.
—is able to talk confidently in public.
—likes doing things with and for his family.
—enjoys his own company and can entertain himself easily.
—is skilled at getting people to express their views and talk about themselves.
—is patient when explaining things to others.
—is able to type sixty words a minute on a word processor.

Next, on a new sheet of paper, write at the top of the page: *How do I know I possess this quality or skill?* Then, write down the first quality or skill that is not self-evident. With the examples above it would be *is able to talk confidently in public.* Concerning the item you wrote down, provide evidence to support your claim of possessing that quality or skill. Go through this procedure for all the relevant items on your list, using a separate sheet of paper for each item.

The main value of this part of the exercise is to convince yourself, with proof, that the positive characteristics you see in the mirror are real, not figments of your imagination. Another benefit is that it forces you to abandon beliefs about yourself that may indeed be illusions. For example, if you cannot offer evidence that you can speak confidently before a group, then it is nothing more than a wish or an unsubstantiated belief and, therefore, should be taken off this list.

To strengthen your beliefs concerning your positive features, bring your list to your best friend and ask the person to help you with this project. You may say something like this: "I'm involved in a personal growth project that requires your help. I chose you because I know you'll be totally honest with me. These are the positive qualities and skills I see in myself. For each one I'd like you to tell me whether or not you agree. If you agree, tell me your reasons; if you don't agree I would also like your reasons. I promise to just listen and not defend myself if I don't see it the way you do."

Be sure to take notes on what this person says and hold on to them.

Students of mine who are sincere about getting to know themselves tell me, after going through this part of the exercise, that they feel much better about themselves once they realize the extent and depth of their qualities. How do *you* feel after completing step one?

STEP TWO

Answer this question: "*What qualities or skills would I like to see in myself (qualities and skills I wish I had) that I now lack?*" Again, use a separate line for each quality and skill, and be specific.

Examples:

I'd like to improve my ability to talk in front of groups.

I want to improve my memory so that I can recall names of people to whom I am introduced.

I'd like to learn to be more patient and not rush things more quickly than they can develop.

After completing this list, write the first one on a separate sheet of paper and answer these questions fully:

1. What *specifically* must I do to develop this?

2. What resources do I need to help me do it?

3. Do I really want to put forth the time and effort to develop it?

4. (Answer only if you wrote yes for question three.) What will I gain if I fulfill this objective? That is, what do I envision as payoffs for putting forth the effort to achieve this?

Do this for each quality or skill you listed. When you complete this part of the project, one of two things will happen: First, you may find a road that will lead you to your objective. Second, you may realize that your desires are not attainable now, or may not be attainable at all considering the effort you must put forth.

This two-step process, when completed, will enable you to clarify who you are and what realistically you must do to develop qualities or skills you lack but consider important.

Assessing Accomplishments

While the exercise you just did is beneficial, you need to do another two-step exercise to help you gain confidence in using the powers you possess.

Again, find a quiet place so you can think about yourself without interruptions.

STEP ONE

Think of *all* your accomplishments, both personal and business. On a blank sheet of paper, describe and number each one. Again, be specific and include anything that remotely sounds like an achievement—something you're proud of—

even if you believe that anyone could have done it. Once you've completed this list, go to step two.

STEP TWO

Write each accomplishment at the top of separate sheets of paper. Then, for each accomplishment you listed, answer these questions in detail:

1. What *personal qualities* enabled me to accomplish this?

2. What *skills* enabled me to accomplish this?

The aim of this exercise is for you to realize what it took to accomplish what you did. That realization should bring you to the conclusion that you must still possess the qualities and skills required to do those things. Assuming you did not mention them in step one of the first exercise, this exercise enabled you to discover more hidden treasures. Congratulations.

But those treasures are worthless unless you use them. You need to find a way of activating your potential, of charging up the Wizard within you. You can't do it by thinking about doing it or by talking about doing it. You have to empower yourself to use your strengths; you have to act.

Many years ago, I heard Dr. Abraham Lowe, who was a well-known Viennese psychiatrist, tell an audience he was addressing, "When you are depressed, you must move your muskles" (not muscles, but musKles, emphasizing the *k*). That is sound advice for anyone whose abilities are dormant. It is also good advice when you are "down" because things are not going as well for you as you would like and you experience intellectual paralysis. When that happens, force yourself to do something, anything, just to get your muskles moving.

With all the positive things you now know about yourself, and all the directions available to you, is there any reason not to move *your* muskles?

10. Beware when false pride dictates your actions; replace it with genuine pride.

In the name of pride, not genuine pride but false pride, many people inadvertently sabotage themselves.

Genuine pride is the sense of self-respect you get from doing the right things or from being the best you can be. It's the "I-feel-good-about-myself" pleasure and satisfaction you get from your accomplishments, from making wise decisions, and from fulfilling meaningful objectives. Your desire to perpetuate those positive feelings, to grow in whatever ways you deem important, and to excel are the forces that motivate behaviors that lead to genuine pride.

False pride, however, is a defensive reaction primarily motivated by one's *extreme* concern over image—how one's actions will be viewed by others. Consider, for example, each of the following reactions to a common situation, and answer this question: Does the reaction reflect genuine pride or false pride?

SITUATION I: You had a disagreement with a close relative or friend and ended the phone conversation feeling angry, vowing not to talk to the person until you got an apology. A week goes by and still you receive no apology. You're tempted to call and make a sincere effort to resolve the disagreement and revive the relationship. But you do not yield to the temptation because you tell yourself, "I don't want to come across as being weak and to give the impression that I gave in."

SITUATION II: Your boss gives you an assignment. Following his detailed explanation, you are puzzled by a couple of elements. So you ask yourself, "Should I ask him to clarify the issues that concern me or should I keep trying to figure them out myself?" The debate with yourself concludes with a decision not to ask. Why? Because you fear that if you do he will think less of you for asking "dumb questions."

SITUATION III: You're driving with a friend to a dinner party. The route is unfamiliar and you are running late. Your friend says, "I think we should go to a gas station and get some directions." You reply, "I don't have to ask anyone; I can find my own way."

All three responses to the situations are examples of *false* pride. If the persons facing those problems had *genuine* pride they would do what was necessary to solve their problems, rather than fearing how their actions would affect their image. First they would ask themselves, "What do I really want? What is most important to me?" Their answers would prompt them to do the *appropriate* things, which would result in outcomes they could genuinely be proud of.

In the first situation, the person should reason, "I want to maintain the good relationship I have always enjoyed. To do that I'll make the call and do everything in my power to get this relationship back on track." In the second situation the thinking should be: "I want to be sure that I fully understand what I'm supposed to do so I can do it right. Whether or not my questions are viewed as dumb is not as relevant as fulfilling my obligations correctly. Perhaps it's better that he *think* I'm dumb than for me to eliminate his doubt by doing the assignment incorrectly." And in the third situation the person should say, "Getting to the dinner party as quickly as possible is what's most important. What difference does it make what the gas-station attendant thinks of me as long as I get to where I want to go?"

How can you prevent false pride from dictating your actions? When in doubt about what action to take, make it a habit to ask yourself two questions: (1) What do I *really* want, i.e., what is most important to me? (2) Will this action (the action you're thinking of taking) lead me to that want? Those questions, answered honestly, will set you on the right course.

Honesty will prompt you to ask for advice when you need it, go for professional help when you need to, ask for opinions from people you respect, admit you are wrong when you are, apologize when it's appropriate, ask questions when you are unsure, and do what's necessary, regardless of how it may appear to others, to fulfill your meaningful wants.

Although I would not minimize the importance of developing and perpetuating a positive image, realize that your image is based more on your actions than anything else. If you want to be viewed as dependable, keep your promises and don't make promises you can't keep. If you want to be liked, be pleasant and act responsibly. If you want people to respect and trust you, be respectable and trustworthy. In short, *do not manufacture an image of yourself with false pride. Rather, let the image evolve through actions that lead you to worthy objectives—those you can genuinely be proud of.*

11. Focus on being and doing your best, not on pleasing others.

Ask any professional athlete, musician, actor, or speaker, "When you perform your skill, what is most important to you, the thing you are doing or the people who pay to see or hear you?" All of them will tell you essentially the same thing: they focus on what they are doing. Knowing that they cannot please *every* person in the audience, they are motivated to focus their energies on pleasing the only ones they know how to please—themselves. They will also tell you that by pleasing themselves they usually satisfy most people in their audience. If you were also to ask them how they please themselves, each would tell you, "By doing the very best job I know how."

As a speaker who has given thousands of talks and presentations, I share those beliefs. Although most of my presentations have been well received, a few I gave early in my career "bombed." The reason for each disaster, I later learned, was essentially the same: I was more concerned with the people I was addressing—how *they* would react and whether *they* would like me—than with my talk. Prior to each poor presentation, I kept thinking that I must satisfy *them,* and hoped *they* would be pleased with me and my messages. What I hadn't realized was this: concentrating on doing my best makes sense, since this process is within my control; worrying about other people's reactions, over which I have no direct control, does not make sense.

Let me tell you when and how I learned this valuable lesson. Just moments before I was to make my maiden appearance on a television show to promote one of my earlier books, the producer, sensing my nervousness, came up to me and said, "You seem uptight. What's the problem?"

I replied, "I've never been on television before. My hands are clammy and my throat is dry. I'm afraid I'll blow it."

"Listen, is there anyone in this studio or any viewer you can imagine who knows more about what you'll be discussing than you?" he asked.

"No," I said.

"All right, then. Concentrate on what you know best and just talk to the host as if he's in your office. Be as convincing and enthusiastic in your conversation with him as you are in your writing. The people watching and listening to you want to know how your ideas will benefit them; they want to know how to make their life better. Nothing else, other than providing them with that knowledge, matters. Nothing."

He said one more thing that made an indelible impression on me. "And remember this. If you strongly believe in your ideas, view them as valuable gifts that you want to share with others."

When I finally took my place in the guest's chair, I was oblivious to everyone and everything, except the host and his questions. All I cared about was giving him my "gifts," the ideas contained in my book. The show came off well—well enough for me to be reinvited several times.

If impressing other people is high on your list of priorities, realize that the harder you try to please others the less chance you have of achieving that objective. It's no different than trying *too* hard to accomplish anything: your emotions, particularly fear of failure, get in your way and you become tense, exercise poor judgment both with your words and actions, and eventually trip yourself up. Trying too hard is another example of a positive quality, trying, carried to an extreme.

Can you imagine if a surgeon, just before conducting an operation, were to think, *I hope I don't do anything to destroy my image; I hope this patient will like me?* That's ludicrous, you say.

Of course, and isn't it just as ridiculous for you to misdirect your energies worrying about how you are perceived? Realize that by assuming a defensive posture, which is evidenced in fear of failure, you not only deplete your energy supply but also cause others to doubt your abilities.

To help you change your focus from pleasing others to being and doing your best, let's first review the logic behind the principle that is the title of this section. I suggest you read this aloud:

I have a desire to be liked by people I deem important.

I feel that by pleasing those people they will like me.

Since I can't *make* them like me, how can I increase my chances of having my desire to be liked fulfilled?

I can give these people what *they* want from me.

What do these people want from me?

They want the *best of me:* my products, services, efforts, or anything of value I have to offer.

If I give them what they want, chances are they *will* like me.

For evidence of this logic, let us examine how *you* form your likes and dislikes toward others. Think of someone you genuinely like. With that person in mind, answer this question: What does this person do for you emotionally, intellectually, physically, or financially that causes you to like him or her? That is, how does this person make you feel in any of those four areas? Repeat this exercise as many times as you want, keeping in mind different people you like. Chances are, you discovered that you like people who do things that make you feel good in one or several ways.

Realize that other people form likes and dislikes toward you the same way you do toward them.

For further evidence that being liked is a function of how you make people feel and that this feeling is based on what you do for them, do this two-part exercise:

1. Recall a specific time when you said to yourself, "I like you." Or, if you didn't actually say those words, you had this strong feeling about yourself. With that time in mind, write down things that happened to bring about that feeling.

2. Next, think of a specific time when you said to yourself, "I don't like you," or something to that effect. Keeping in mind that time, write down the events that triggered that feeling.

Are you now convinced that it's what you *do*, whether it's for others or for yourself, that determines how likeable you are? These exercises are further proof that doing your best is the only reasonable route to pleasing others, since they use the same criteria for determining the extent to which they like you.

In conclusion, wanting to please others is fine, as long as it is not your focus and does not take precedence over pleasing yourself by doing your best. When it does take precedence, you lose sight of the only thing over which you have control—your efforts.

To make sure you focus on doing your best, rather than on pleasing others, ask yourself: What are the gifts I want to give to others? Of what value will these gifts be to them? If you are convinced that your gifts will be of value to the people you share them with, you will not worry about their reactions, over which you have no control.

12. Avoid the "nice guy" trap;
be forthright with yourself and others.

You have seen how false pride and overconcern with pleasing others can prevent you from achieving results that really matter.

Now I'll introduce you to another quality that is potentially more damaging than either of those. It is the "nice guy" syndrome.

"Nice guys" are mainly motivated by their desire for *everyone* to like them. Harold, who is affable and on the surface appears to be responsible, personified this type of individual. Although he was preoccupied with being liked and with making favorable impressions on others, he frequently failed to achieve either desire. Probably his failures were a direct result of his preoccupations.

Harold was a bright, good-looking, thirty-five-year-old assistant human-resource director at a large pharmaceutical firm. His words, assuring others of his eagerness to be of service, as well as his pleasant demeanor belied his actions. Specifically, he almost never turned down requests, regardless of how unreasonable they were. Believing he'd be disliked if he did refuse, he invariably overcommitted himself. For example, he promised to complete projects by certain dates, even though he knew he could not possibly deliver. And because of his unrealistic promises, he often turned in reports late and showed up late for meetings, even important ones.

Harold also volunteered for company-sponsored charity events, just so others would think well of him and say how wonderful and unselfish he was. But, as was characteristic of him, at the last minute he frequently reneged on his commitments, disappointing the people who counted on him. Sometimes he completely forgot about his promises. But, when reminded of them, he apologized profusely, claiming he was too busy to honor those commitments and too busy to tell anyone he couldn't follow through.

Developing a reputation for being irresponsible and untrustworthy, Harold became known as someone who "talked a better game than he played." His "nice guy" gestures resulted in him finally being fired. Several years later I discovered that he lost two subsequent jobs; I suspect for the same reasons.

Pleasing others and not wanting to hurt people's feelings are the main reasons many "nice guys" give for not saying no, even when it's appropriate. Those are also the reasons they give for making unreasonable promises. What happens when a "nice guy" fails to fulfill a commitment? Generally, he offers an excuse for why he couldn't do it or faults the people who make the request for being unreasonably demanding. Then he makes another empty promise.

If "nice guys" were *genuinely* nice and truly concerned with others, they would not, as they often do, kill others with their kindness: keeping people dangling, anticipating, and guessing, all because they don't want to be bearers of bad news, news that might tarnish their image and possibly cause others to dislike them.

Rich was such a person. He rose to his position of quality-control manager because he succeeded in giving the false impression of being a good manager of people. Actually, in his climb to this responsible position, he left a trail of hurt, disillusioned, angry, and unemployed people. For example, when he was disappointed and upset with employees who performed below his expectations, he typically said nothing to them. Rather than show them what was wrong and how they could improve, he fretted and complained to others about their poor performance.

When I asked why he doesn't say anything to the people who aren't producing, he said, "Because I don't want to offend them. My employees like me; I wouldn't want to do anything to destroy that feeling."

"How do you get them to improve?" I asked.

"I don't," he said. "I let them hang themselves. They eventually realize they are not cut out for this work and they quit."

Even when his subordinates requested guidance and he promised to help them, he rarely had time or patience to do it. Actually, he was concerned that people would not respond well to his instruction. So, he kept putting them off until it was too late.

Probably the ugliest action of "nice guys" is their brick collecting. Phil was an expert at it, both at work, where it cost him potentially good, loyal employees, and at home, where it cost him his marriage.

This is how Phil operated at work: If someone did or said something that offended him, he wouldn't say anything. His reason? Just like Rich, he did not want to hurt anyone's feelings. Also, he could not tolerate confrontations. Although he said nothing, he filed the act in his brain; it was the start of his brick collection. If that person did something offensive again, he collected another brick. And so it went until he accumulated enough bricks to do one of two things, depending upon his feelings toward the person. Sometimes, when he gathered enough bricks to justify an attack, he hurled them, accusing the offender of all sorts of bad things he or she had done, and blaming the person for all the suffering these actions caused. Other times he built invisible walls, which ultimately resulted in him firing the person or persons whose actions prompted the brick collection.

The only clue people in Phil's department had that he was building a wall was when he stopped talking to the person who was the object of his wrath. When that person asked if there was anything wrong, Phil would say, "Nothing's wrong." Yet he'd continue to collect bricks instead of voicing his anger. Only when Phil felt justified in firing someone did he tell the person all the reasons for his action. Of course, the evidence was too overwhelming for anything constructive to be done about it.

He ended his twelve-year marriage to his wife, Margaret, the same way he terminated work relationships. The beginning of the end came two years before the divorce. He first stopped sharing work-related and other personal information with her. When she asked him what was new or for updates on specific activities she knew about, he would respond with one- or two-word answers. Later, he found reasons not to come home for dinner as regularly as he had in the past. And so it went. Sensing that her marriage was in trouble, Margaret confronted Phil with her concerns and suggested they seek help. For approximately a year and a half he kept denying there was a problem. At times he would accuse Margaret of imagining things.

Then, following one of their arguments, which were becoming more frequent, he told her that he wanted a divorce. When she asked him how long he had been unhappy and why he hadn't told her what was bothering him, he said, "I've been miserable for about two years. I didn't tell you because I didn't want to hurt your feelings."

"And what do you think you're doing now and have been doing for the past two years?" she asked.

According to Margaret, he had no response to that question. But the wall he built was so thick and tall there was no way out of the situation other than a divorce. As for Margaret, she was just another victim of his "nice guy" behaviors.

Many "nice guys," under the guise of wanting to be helpful, also meddle in people's affairs, give unsolicited advice, and do things for others without obtaining their consent. "I know what's best for you," "I just wanted to help," or "I didn't want to hurt your feelings" are common justifications for their actions. These seemingly altruistic motives are, for the most part, self-centered, and inconsiderate of other people's desires or interests. A truly altruistic person does not *impose* his or her sensibilities and desires on others.

Since they are not forthright with themselves and others, "nice guys" can't be trusted. How can anyone be trusted if his or her main motive for saying and doing things is to avoid disagreement or to avoid being disliked? How can you trust anyone who says yes but whose actions say no? How can you trust anyone who lacks the courage to be the messenger of bad news? In short, how can you trust someone whose actions are primarily motivated by defensiveness? Obviously you can't, and neither can anyone else.

If you have an inordinate need to be liked and to please others, and that need has the potential of being harmful to yourself and others, consider the following guidelines and advice, which will help you reorient your thinking and direct you on a more productive course:

Most people prefer forthrightness and sincerity even though it may inconvenience them. They would, for example, prefer that you decline a request, rather than grudgingly agree and resent them later for asking.

People can accept legitimate refusals. They prefer them to the disappointments of unkept promises. If you can't honor a request, say so rather than keep people wondering, waiting, and hoping.

People will not like you less for being sincere and honest with them, so long as you temper those qualities with good judgment; by being tactful you can mitigate most emotional and intellectual pains.

People will respect you for tactfully leveling with them. More important, you will increase your respect for yourself when you accept tasks you can do and reject those you can't. Doing so creates the impression that your actions speak as loudly as your words.

Realize that others have a right to know the truth, regardless of how painful it may be; don't protect them from reality.

Don't impose your help on others. Genuine nice guys respect people's desires to lead their own lives.

In short, *you'll be better liked if you don't try so hard to be liked. Realize that genuine nice guys are more interested in being good than in looking good.*

13. Reduce your excessive dependencies.

When we enter this world, we are totally dependent and, therefore, not in control of our lives. When we leave it, or just before we do, we again are totally dependent and lack control of our lives. Between these two major events, much of what we do that's important is motivated by our need to decrease our dependencies and increase our independence. The extent to which we succeed in doing both is a measure of how much control we have over our lives.

Our need to be in control, i.e., to be able to *make* things happen or to influence outcomes, is the driving force behind our desire for education, training, and money. All three of those assets increase our self-reliance and serve as tools to do more of the kinds of things we *want* to do. The more specialized or advanced our education or training, and the more money we possess, the greater our options and opportunities to achieve our objectives. In short, being in control enables us to do whatever it takes to feel good about ourselves physically, emotionally, and intellectually.

While having control increases our self-reliance and, therefore, is worth striving for, it is impossible to be *totally* independent. You can, however, strive to reduce any *excessive dependencies* you may have, those that control you. Excessive dependencies have a stranglehold on you. They limit your options and prevent you from exercising free will. For example, a person who is excessively dependent on alcohol generally is intellectually, physically, and/or emotionally incapacitated until that dependency is satisfied. Such a person is obviously controlled by his or her dependence on alcohol.

Here is another example of how an excessive dependency can control you. Suppose you owned a company and you had one customer or client who represented 80 percent of your revenue. If you were to lose that client, and there were no other to take his place, you would, for all practical purposes, be out of business. Because that client knows you are at his mercy, isn't he controlling you?

In short, whenever someone or something is the sole source of your emotional, intellectual, or financial sustenance, you are being controlled by that person or thing. That's like the proverbial tail wagging the dog. To prevent or overcome this uncomfortable state, you must take steps to reduce those dependencies that run your life and, at the same time, increase your options for achieving your desires. Before doing this, you have to identify the nature of your excessive dependencies.

The Nature of Excessive Dependencies

Excessive dependencies fall into two categories:

1. *Addictions of any sort.* That's when reliance on chemicals, work, or people is so extreme that without them life is meaningless. These addictions arise from emotional and/or biochemical forces that overpower our judgment. We don't consciously develop these dependencies; they just happen. A person doesn't say, for example, I want to become so addicted to my job that without it I am nothing. Nor does anyone say, I so desperately need the approval of others that without it I cannot function. Yet those, in effect, are the kinds of statements that people possessing such addictions make. Each person views the thing on which he is dependent as the center of his universe—the driving force of his life. He is like the mythical king Midas, who was so consumed with gold that it almost destroyed him. And so it is with all addictions; they have the potential to destroy us.

2. *Fears of any sort.* Every fear—whether it is fear of the unknown, fear of failure, fear of losing one's main source of income, fear of losing a major source of emotional support, or fear of saying or doing the wrong things—creates dependencies. The more intense the fear, the greater the dependence. A case in point involves a five-person department of a local bank. The people constantly went to their manager, Jason, with questions concerning projects they were working on. Even when they knew the answers to their questions, they still asked him what to do. It got to the point that he spent so much time answering questions and telling his people what to do that he had little time for his own work.

   At one of the department's meetings he broached the problem. In effect he said, I know you know the answers to many of the questions you ask. How come you ask me anyway? After some hemming and hawing, they finally told him that they were afraid of being wrong. They told him that in the past he yelled at them when they erred or made a decision he did not agree with. To protect themselves against such reactions, they considered it safer just to ask rather than take the risk of being wrong.

Defensive reactions, such as those Jason triggered, are typical with anything we fear. Why? Because fears cause us to distrust our judgment. They also cause us to be needy. In short, the more afraid we are, *the more needy we are; the less fearful we are, the more self-sufficient we are.* (And as for Jason, who inspires all this fear and defensiveness, he would do well to examine Principles 20, 22, and 23 in the next chapter and modify the way he deals with his staff. These principles focus on listening and speaking without judging.)

Notice, with both types of excessive dependencies, people mainly rely on external forces either to maintain or restore balance in their lives. That is, they are dependent on other people or things, rather than on their inner resources, for their happiness or satisfaction.

How to Reduce
Your Excessive Dependencies

My aim for the balance of this section is to show you how to reduce those dependencies that interfere with your ability to feel good about yourself physically, emotionally, and intellectually. Like all other growth experiences this takes time and effort. But if you follow these instructions, you will succeed.

First, on paper, perhaps in the notebook you used in earlier exercises, describe in detail any addictions you have that cause you to feel less than good about yourself *physically*. Two examples might be: I eat too much junk food, particularly candy bars; I spend too much time watching television and feel like a couch potato. Title this page *Excessive Physical Dependencies*.

Next, on a separate sheet of paper titled *Excessive Emotional and Intellectual Dependencies,* describe those behaviors and attitudes that fall into both categories. Some examples are: I get *overly* concerned with what other people think of me; I *desperately* need others to tell me I'm worthy before I can feel worthy myself; Without the *constant* presence of other people I feel lost; Since *my work is my life,* I spend more time doing it than I actually want; *I live for my children*—without them life is meaningless.

Finally, on another sheet of paper, write at the top of the page, *I am extremely afraid of_____.* Then, complete the sentence with statements that express fears you would like to overcome. For example, I am extremely afraid of computers. I am especially afraid of doing something that might cause me to lose information. I am also extremely afraid of losing my job. And I am extremely afraid of saying anything that might cause others to dislike me.

By completing these lists, you have taken the first step to increasing control of your life, since awareness is the beginning of change. To actually make the changes, you need to decide what specific dependencies you want to work on and then develop a plan for achieving your objectives. I urge you not to work on more than two or three dependencies at a time; these are difficult enough to overcome without compounding your mission by overloading yourself.

Once you decide which dependencies or fears you want to overcome, list each on separate sheets of paper using the following heading: *Specific Steps or Actions I Must Take to Reduce My Addiction to or Fear of* (whatever addiction or fear you chose to work on). Then, before you list the action steps, write down *all* the reasons for wanting to make this commitment to yourself. When you are fully convinced of the benefits you will gain from following through on the plan, go ahead and list the steps you need to take to accomplish each objective.

The reason why *you* must come up with the plan is that there are so many different addictions and fears, as well as personalities, that no single approach, no universal plan, works for every problem or every person. To increase the likelihood of succeeding, consider the following three thoughts:

1. To overcome an addiction effectively, you have to replace it with something else that is better for you. For example, if you're addicted to work, you might want to replace this addiction with one or two hobbies that provide you with personal satisfaction.

2. Since it is difficult to overcome addictions and fears, you would be wise to consider enlisting the aid of groups, organizations, or professionals who can help you through the rough times.

3. All methods of increasing control of your life, both those you come up with and others discussed in subsequent sections, require you to develop habits that may be foreign to you. Since habits, good or bad, stubbornly resist change, you cannot take a casual approach. The dogged resistance of any bad habit has to be fought with resolve and commitment, strong enough and consistent enough to overpower it. Don't take lightly the tenacity of the bad habits you want to replace. Defeat them with good habits, possibly using the tools discussed under Principle 6.

Since you are vibrant and, therefore, not ready to leave this world, doesn't it make sense to do all you can to increase control of your life? It's all up to you.

14. Concerning each thing you must do, tell yourself, "I *want* to do it," rather than, "I *should* do it."

For a moment, activate your imagination and picture a "Should," as in *I should do this thing that people expect or that my conscience urges me to do. This is not a thing I necessarily like to do, but if I don't do it I'll feel guilty.* What does this "Should" look like? What is it doing and saying?

Based on the responses of many people to whom I posed those questions, I have come up with a composite picture that I'd like to share with you. The particular "Should" I am referring to is a nondescript little character, a part of your conscience, that sits on either shoulder. It is pushing, urging, and nagging you to do things you've been postponing because you'd rather not do them, like phoning or writing a letter to a relative or friend, or cleaning your desk or your bedroom, or expressing your disappointment in someone's actions or job performance.

Although you feel you have to do these things, you tend to resist giving in to your "Shoulds" and procrastinate fulfilling those obligations for as long as you can. Why? Because they're either not fun to do or they are, for reasons only you know, low on your priority list. Since "Shoulds" are persistent, they don't give up their struggles with you. Eventually, when you tire of fighting, you resentfully satisfy their demands. (Before you read on, think of several current "Shoulds" that are gnawing at you. Write them down on a sheet of paper, beginning each one with "I should." We'll get back to this list later.)

As you know, these "Shoulds" can be heavy burdens. They can drain you of energy you could use more productively, and if you let them, they will control your life and weigh you down. Since they are persistent, think of how much more peaceful your life could be if you could rid yourself of all your burdensome "Shoulds" and replace them with "Wants." Consider, for example, the difference in how you feel when you telephone someone because you *should* as opposed to calling because you *want to.*

The moment you convince yourself that the things you *have* to do are also what you *want* to do, you are in charge of your actions. Admittedly, it's a mind game, but it works if you are sincere.

A friend of mine told me how he uses this principle to

remain on his exercise program. When, after recovering from a mild heart attack, he began his physician-prescribed, three-times-a-week exercise routine at the health club, he did it because he felt he should. His doctor told him that unless he exercised regularly he would be vulnerable to another heart attack. For the first six months of his exercise program he resented the time it took out of his schedule. He hated it so much that he almost quit.

After we discussed his "should problem," he agreed that *choosing* to exercise would be more palatable to him than viewing this necessity as an obligation imposed by his physician. He promised to try this approach. When I saw him a couple weeks following our discussion, he told me, "Now that I've changed my attitude toward exercising, I actually *want* to exercise and even look forward to it." When I asked him what he looked forward to he said, "I anticipate feeling good after completing my routine, taking a shower, and then rewarding myself with breakfast before I go to work."

You can employ a similar strategy with other "must," seemingly unappealing activities. As long as you have to do them, it doesn't make sense to fight yourself by making it a "Should" or by telling yourself how much you dislike doing it. Just do it. To increase your motivation, think of the benefits you will gain from accomplishing what you have to do. Think of ways to make the task more pleasant. Do whatever it takes to make the process bearable. Then, *just do it.*

When our four children were living at home, they were each charged with certain responsibilities. Some they accepted without fuss, but others triggered negative reactions. Taking out the garbage was dreaded most by all the children and, therefore, produced the greatest resistance. The dialogue between my wife, Joan, and each child was short and to the point. It began with Joan pleading, "Would you please take out the garbage?" "I don't like taking out the garbage," came the whining reply. Joan said, "I'm not asking you to like it. Just do it." Joan had the last word, the discussion was over, and the garbage went out.

They each learned, after several such encounters, the fruitlessness of resisting what inevitably will be.

Her point made a lot of sense. Liking to do something you have to do is a luxury. If we insist on liking everything we do before doing it, much of what we must do would not get done.

Make all your must actions *your* choices by convincing yourself that you want to do them. Let's try it with *your* list of "Shoulds." With each one answer the following questions:

> "If I do this 'should,' how will I benefit?"

> "How can I make this thing I have to do more bearable?"

> "How else can I convince myself that I really *want* to do it?"

Once you get into the habit of asking yourself those questions, you won't think about "Shoulds" or consider whether or not you like doing what's required of you. Rather, you will just do whatever has to get done because you believe it's necessary. You will *want* to do things you have to do rather than feel victimized by a pushy "Should." You will also reduce the distractions and the burdens of battling yourself.

It's no accident that Nike, a major athletic-wear company, has adopted a slogan that has become a catch phrase since they introduced it. The phrase is *"just do it."* It's no accident because as a practical cure for putting off doing things we must do, even if we don't like to do them, it simply makes sense, just as it did when Joan introduced it when our children were young.

15. To overpower your fear of failure, take one step at a time; reward yourself for each successful step you take.

If you were absolutely certain that everything you said or did would be well received and that all your decisions were right decisions, chances are you would substantially diminish your fear of saying or doing things. You would confidently offer suggestions and opinions, embrace interesting challenges that test your skills and intellect, and take risks that pushed your limits beyond what you thought possible. In short, you would make creative use of your freedom and take advantage of the opportunities that most wise, fearless, and courageous people enjoy.

But, since we do not live in a judgment-free world, you, like many other people, may be afraid that your statements and actions will be judged unfairly or wrongly or that your abilities are not good enough to fulfill your desires. When present, such fears prevent you from taking risks associated with new and tough challenges, engaging in competition, making decisions, setting high expectations, and sustaining a high level of performance.

Such fear-based reactions, which stem from low self-esteem, are often triggered by painful memories of past failures and unfortunate experiences. Because those memories play havoc with your confidence, they stimulate such negative self-talk as "I can't," "I don't know how," "Maybe I'm not as good as I thought," "What if I'm wrong?" "What if it doesn't turn out right?" "I'm sure I'll be rejected," "What if I fail?" and so on. They are voices of ghosts from the past, revisiting you every time you are about to embark on a difficult and demanding activity or project. So, just like children who avoid tasks at which they have failed or that have caused them embarrassment, you dignify old disappointing experiences and allow them to victimize you and scare you into either avoiding risks or fulfilling your negative prophecies.

It's time to bury those ghosts, whoever they are and wherever they came from, and develop the confidence you need to move forward. A good way to start is to make your goals easily attainable. Instead of *focusing* on the "bottom line," i.e., the achievement of an ultimate goal or a final product, focus your energies on each step that leads to a goal. View the achievement of each step as your measure of success. In so doing, you not only succeed every time you take a step, but with each step you increase your confidence.

Each completed step is proof of your abilities and gives you the courage to take the next step, the step after that, and so on. You soon realize that basically *your* actions alone, the forward steps *you* take, are producing the results you want. Although you may give credit to luck and providence, you can thank yourself for being the major contributor to your achievements.

Try it. Set a specific goal for yourself, and make it one that's worth pursuing—one that will contribute to your physical, intellectual, emotional, or financial well-being. In your notebook, which by this time should be filling up, write down a goal you want to pursue. Next, write down all the steps you have to take to achieve that goal. When you describe the steps, be specific.

For example, let us say you set the following goal: "I want to improve my ability to talk in front of large groups." That being a reasonable goal, the following steps will lead you to it.

> Locate a reputable teaching institution or facility that offers such a course or program. Make sure it is consistent with your budget and the amount of time you want to devote to this effort. Three options are private facilities such as those frequently advertised in newspapers, community colleges, and a local chapter of Toastmasters International.

> Register for the course or program that you decide is right for you.

> Consistently do the assignments required of you.

> In addition to your major goal that prompted you to register for this course or program, set subgoals that, when reached, will serve as evidence that you are progressing toward your main goal.

To strengthen your belief that your actions will lead you to your desired destination, endorse yourself, literally pat yourself on the back, each time you have completed a step or substep toward your goal. Tell yourself: "That successful step is solid evidence that I have what it takes to take the next step toward my goal; I have proven to myself that I have nothing to fear."

Another way of gaining confidence is to practice regularly that which you lack confidence in doing. Practice enables you to gain trust in your ability to employ consistently the desired quality or skill. Once you decide on a particular goal, commit yourself to practice the skills consistently until they become automatic. This is no different than developing new habits; consistent practice is what it takes to make them part of you.

Joe, an accountant who started taking piano lessons at age fifty, was so self-conscious of his abilities that he would not allow anyone to hear him play, including his wife and grown children. When he practiced, he always made sure nobody was around. Not until he learned a piece so well that he could play it error free from memory did he feel confident to perform it. But, to accomplish that feat, he practiced a piece hundreds of times. While he had no hopes of becoming a concert pianist, his efforts built his confidence sufficiently to play occasionally for his wife, children, and grandchildren.

Although there are no shortcuts to overcoming fear of failure, by incorporating the following thoughts and guidelines into your life you'll have a good start:

1. A person who hasn't withstood and overcome continues to feel doubtful that he or she could. To reduce that doubt you must take the risks turtles take when they stick their necks and limbs out of their shells. Without taking that risk you cannot move forward.

2. Failure is talking yourself out of trying. Success is a process that gains momentum and strength with each forward step you take. It's a process that fills you with confidence. The sooner you embark on that process the quicker you'll achieve success, however you define it.

3. When in doubt about whether or not to take a risk, tell yourself, "If I take the risk, I may face certain adverse consequences, but I also could realize benefits. If I don't

take risks, I have absolutely no chance of achieving what I really want. Not taking appropriate risks is a defensive posture I cannot afford, for it reduces my opportunities."

4. You are not fully in control of outcomes or the "bottom line." However, you do control the process—all the things you must do to achieve the results you want. To put it differently, although you aren't the sole determiner of a game's outcome, you and only you determine how well you play. Playing the game the best you can is being a winner.

5. You will get past your initial fears if you just take the first step. You will reduce much of your fear by taking each subsequent step *one at a time.*

To gear yourself up for taking reasonable risks and, in doing so, overpowering your fear of failure, reread these guidelines frequently until you believe them.

16. Make specific and reasonable promises to yourself each day; fulfill those promises.

Of course you want to be successful; most of us do. Yet many people despair because they don't see themselves as such. Why? One reason is that they have not achieved those goals they equate with success, such as financial independence, certain possessions, a position they long for, or some other accomplishment that, to them, is concrete evidence of their success.

Another reason is that they've developed a variation of the following self-defeating behavior pattern, so that they inadvertently sabotage themselves when working on long-range goals: *I'll start a project, but once I'm into it I get so bored or bogged down that I quit. Since I feel lousy about myself for quitting, I'll begin another project. And so it goes; I start projects, don't finish them, feel guilty, and soon after I initiate another one.*

By employing the principle that is the title of this section, you will learn how to feel successful regardless of whether or not you achieve the goals you equate with success. In the next principle, which is an extension of this one, you will learn how, if it is a problem, to overcome the self-defeating behaviors described above in italics.

Success, according to the *Random House College Dictionary*, is defined in two ways: first, "the favorable or prosperous termination of attempts," and second, "the attainment of wealth, position, honors, or the like." While the second definition is the more popular, it is limiting. The definition I prefer, which offers more possibilities, yet is not much different than the first, is this: *success is a process of fulfilling specific, meaningful promises to yourself each day.*

That view of success allows you to begin each day, regardless of what happened on the preceding one, with renewed optimism and vigor. All you have to do at the start of each day is create a reasonable things-to-do list for that day, specifying next to each item the amount of time you plan to invest in each activity. If the activity is part of a large project, specify how much of it you want to accomplish. Then, do everything in your power to complete the activities on the list.

At the end of the day look at your list, your promises to yourself, and determine to what extent you succeeded. If you were, say, 80 percent successful that day, that's OK because you have another chance the next day and each day after that. More important, you don't have to wait to accomplish a particular goal before you can look in the mirror and think, I am successful because I promised myself to do these specific things today and I did all of them, or 90 percent of them, or whatever.

Do you see the beauty in that thinking? First, every day offers a new opportunity to succeed because success is a positive termination of a process, which you define as your one day's accomplishments of items on your things-to-do list. Second, success rests in your hands alone, whereas success defined by the achievement of some major goal may require other people's approval and reactions, neither of which you can directly control. Third, you can enjoy the feeling of success if you do everything in your power to fulfill whatever obligations you assume, regardless of the outcome.

By making reasonable promises to yourself every day and fulfilling them, you will not only increase control of your life but you'll also enjoy the success that control provides.

17. View the completion of each step toward a long-range goal as a fruit of your labor.

If, like many people, you are obsessed with "bottom lines," you may be denying yourself benefits stemming from the process that leads to your goals. With long-range projects and goals, the steps leading to your final destination are not only important but can be at least as satisfying as achieving the goal itself. And, like planning a party, excursion, or vacation, the process can also be fun, often as much fun as the event itself.

To meet each long-range goal you must go through three phases: a beginning, middle, and end. Beginnings are fun and exciting. Starting school, beginning a new position, getting married, giving birth, and embarking on any ambitious undertaking are all spirit-lifting events. They are reasons to be proud, to celebrate, and even to boast. It's fun, exhilarating, and good for the soul to be congratulated and complimented when you announce your intent to go on a diet, quit smoking, write a book, pursue a degree, go into business for yourself, or whatever. Once you have begun your project, other people's enthusiasm toward it diminishes. And when you enter the next phase—the middle or the process leading to your goal—you are on your own.

After the initial "That's great," "Congratulations," "I'm really proud of you," the next time you can anticipate such fervor from others is when you've fulfilled your commitment, reached your destination, or delivered your promise. Why? Because most people are not interested in the details and travails of your "pregnancy"; they want to see the baby. They don't care what you have to go through to get to the "bottom line"; they just want to see the results of your efforts.

It could be a long time, often more than nine months, between your announcement of your undertaking and the final results you hope to achieve. It could be a long time before anyone applauds your accomplishment, tells you what a great job you've done, or compliments you for fulfilling your promise—probably longer than you would like.

To ward off impatience and to maintain enthusiasm for the long haul, you have to have a strategy that places you in control of your satisfaction and the compliments you receive while working on the project. That strategy begins by dividing the project into subgoals, as many as you'd like, and celebrating the achievement of each.

At the start of your project, write down the exact steps you must take to get from where you are to your final destination; number the steps and keep them in a place that's easily accessible.

While your final destination is indeed your *ultimate* goal, for now make each subgoal—each step—your target, even though these steps are only intermediate targets. The reason is that intermediate objectives are much easier to attain than the larger goal (the end result).

This idea is not new. "One day at a time" has been a major philosophy of one of the most successful helping organizations in the world: Alcoholics Anonymous. Also, achievers in sports will tell you that they do not concentrate on winning, although they may think about it. What they concentrate on is performing to the best of their abilities . . . one point at a time, one stroke at a time, one hole at a time, one basket at a time, or one play at a time. The steps are what's most important to them. Why? Because they know that each step accomplished to the best of their abilities will eventually lead them to their objectives.

Once you accomplish a particular subgoal, celebrate the achievement by patting yourself on the back, either literally or some other way that is satisfying to you. The point is that you're entitled to relish the moment of this small victory. You owe yourself a reward for completing that step. Aside from the fact that you earned it, each subgoal celebration will gear you up for the subsequent one. Eventually you will attain the large victory you are striving for. Equally important, you will enjoy the process, the trip toward your destination, as well as have the satisfaction of the final reward.

Admittedly, it may be difficult to be enthusiastic about doing things that do not yield visible results during every step. Gardening is one such activity. Those who enjoy it know that unless they want a weed patch, they must cultivate, water regularly, weed, and consistently do whatever is necessary to grow beautiful flowers, healthy vegetables, or tasty fruit. While each of their maintenance steps does not produce a concrete outcome, their fervent belief that those actions are essential to achieve the results they desire motivates them to keep at it.

Similarly, to achieve any long-range goal, you must believe and tell yourself often:

1. I must do everything necessary, whether or not I like doing it, to achieve my desired goal.

2. I must pat myself on the back, physically or verbally, each time I do a right thing that gets me closer to my goal.

3. I want to do those two things so I can both enjoy the process that leads to my goal and have a good chance of reaching that goal.

18. Set your standards reasonably high and live by them.

For each of the following pairs of statements, which reflects *your* standards?

A. It's good enough.
B. If something is worth doing it is worthy of my best effort.

A. I didn't have the time, money, and resources to do a decent job.

B. Given the available time, money, and resources, this is the best I can do.

A. As long as I'm doing well, I'm satisfied.
B. I'm doing well, but I keep looking for ways to be better.

A. I'll settle for whatever I can get.
B. I'm entitled to the best and, therefore, will not settle for less.

A. I'll do whatever it takes just to get by.
B. Anyone can get by; I want to do my best so I could feel proud of my efforts.

A. If people mistreat me, I will mistreat them; an eye for an eye, a tooth for a tooth.
B. I treat people the way I would like them to treat me.

If you chose the *B* response for each pair of statements, you are on the road to developing the quality judgments that wise people exercise. You may recall, *a wise person says and does the right things, in the right ways, and in the right times and places.* To uphold high standards as consistently as wise people do, you first have to identify them in both the business and personal dimensions of your life. Specifically, the objective of the next set of exercises is to establish standards—acceptable and unacceptable behaviors—as they relate to:

1. the products or services you generate either at work or at home.

2. the way you treat yourself.

3. the way you treat others.

For each one of those three areas, your objective is to

develop a list of "I will" and "I won't" statements that reflects your desire to be the best you can be. The "I will" statements represent attitudes and actions that you believe are *right*, while the "I won't" statements represent attitudes and actions that you believe are *wrong*. Consider the following example for "the products or services you generate either at work or at home."

I will inspect my work to make sure it's what I want it to be.

I will ask others to check my work to be sure it's as good as I want it to be.

I will be attentive to details, checking and double-checking if necessary.

I will correct anything that needs to be corrected.

I will fulfill all my promises.

I will do everything in my power to make sure people receive the quality service or product they rightfully expect from me.

I will deal with complaints in a responsible manner.

I won't submit anything that represents my "first draft" or less than my best work.

I won't look for excuses to submit substandard work.

I won't disregard complaints leveled against me, my product, or my services.

As you draw up your lists for all three items, remember that you're looking for *reasonably* high standards, not standards that are impossible to achieve or that are so low that they encourage mediocrity. Now, let us look at a sample list of standards for "the way you treat yourself."

I will make reasonable promises to myself daily and do my best to fulfill them.

I will do everything in my power to make the most of today and every other day.

I will be honest with myself and accept well-intentioned criticism.

I will be mindful of what I want by regularly asking myself, "What do I want?" whenever I am confused or at a crossroads.

When I am "down," I will think of ways to get myself out of that state.

I will pat myself on the back when I have done something to earn it.

I won't berate myself, either privately or to others.

I won't wallow in self-pity or in other negative thoughts and emotions that prevent me from moving forward.

Finally, here is a sample of standards for "the way you treat others."

I will treat others, particularly people who are important to me, the way I would like to be treated by them.

I will be honest with people, but I will temper that honesty with sensitive judgment.

I will do everything in my power to help people who want to be helped.

I won't compromise my values or standards just to please others.

I won't hurt people just to benefit me.

After you have completed the three lists that reflect *your* standards, have them readily available so you can review them regularly.

CHAPTER 4

Developing Sound Relationships
with Others

Wise people I have known are decent, caring, and respectful, both toward themselves and others. Those who occupy managerial positions in business organizations bring out the best in others by actually practicing, not merely mouthing, the golden rule. They actually treat others, as well as themselves, the way they would like to be treated. They stand out in their respective companies because they consistently practice those fundamental principles called "common sense" and, in so doing, gain cooperation from people and get the results they are paid to produce.

In their personal lives, their appropriate actions and reactions enable them to develop solid, lasting relationships, the kinds most people wish they had.

In this chapter you will learn how to use all the key interpersonal-relations principles that seem to come naturally to wise people. Specifically, you will learn

—how to show respect to people you deem important,
—how *really* to listen,
—how to learn from criticisms that are leveled at you,

97

—how to take the sting out of criticisms you level at others, and, at the same time, make those criticisms helpful,

—how to say what you mean to say with silence, and

—how to make it easy for people to give you what you want by giving them what they want.

As with all the other principles we discussed earlier, knowing what these principles are is only the first step to gaining wisdom. Using the principles appropriately demonstrates that you actually possess wisdom. To achieve this aim, you must, just as you did with the other principles, make a concerted effort to practice them. Again, nothing of value comes easily. But the rewards you can reap will justify the investment of your time and energy.

19. Be respectful to all people you value.

Life is difficult enough; we don't have to make it tougher for ourselves by alienating people we deem important, whether the relationships are marketing or personal based. Yet many of us do just that when we fail to respect people we value.

Although all the principles in this chapter deal with different ways of demonstrating respect, my purpose in discussing this general principle separately is to highlight the importance of respect and to set the stage for all the other principles relating to it.

The Opposite of Respect

Nobody wants to be taken for granted, since it is an expression of disrespect, and *everyone* wants to be respected because it makes them feel important. Let us first consider the reasons why taking people you value for granted is insulting and, therefore, unwise.

As we discussed earlier, when you take someone for granted, the message you convey is this: No matter how I act toward you, no matter what I say or do, and regardless of how inconsiderate those actions may be, I expect you to give me what I want and need from you. In short, although I expect you to be responsive to my needs, I don't have to do anything special to earn it. This attitude is based on at least three *faulty* assumptions:

1. That the person being taken for granted doesn't mind it.

2. That the person being taken for granted will continue indefinitely to tolerate the insulting treatments.

3. That the person being taken for granted lacks the courage to stand up for him- or herself.

What makes those assumptions faulty is that people may eventually tire of mistreatment and muster the courage to do something about it. In a larger sense, isn't the unwillingness to tolerate mistreatment the cause of revolutions?

Have you ever been taken for granted? How did you feel? Were you resentful, angry, and bitter toward the person whose actions conveyed an "I'm taking you for granted" attitude? Did you also feel used and abused, and were you tempted to sever your relationship with this person? Perhaps you even yielded to that temptation and felt justified in doing so. If you ever had those feelings and ended a relationship because of it, you are not unique. Why? Because being taken for granted violates a basic need all of us have, which is to feel special and to be treated accordingly.

Is it any wonder that most, if not all, failures of important relationships—those of corporate managers and their employees, organizations and their customers, parents and their children, and intimate friends—are the result of one or both parties taking the other for granted? Consider any one of those relationships, for example, an organization and its customers. If you were the customer of a company that *assumed* you would be loyal to it, and, therefore, did not regularly provide you with the service you desired, would you continue doing business with it? Of course not; not if you had a choice.

If your actions fail to consider the other person's feelings, wants, and needs, you inadvertently convey an "I take you for granted" attitude, which, in the long run, will sabotage your chances of gaining cooperation and loyalty from people you value. On the other hand, a respectful attitude, backed by appropriate actions that reflect genuine caring, is likely to increase your chances of others *willingly* giving you what you want.

Developing a Respectful Attitude

RE-SPECT: to look at (*spect*) again (*re*); to give a second thought to; to be considerate of; to view a person worthy of your time, attention, and courtesy; to accept that person's individuality and idiosyncrasies, so long as doing so doesn't adversely affect you. Those are the basic characteristics of a respectful attitude. Failure to respect someone is tantamount to ignoring the person.

Respectful people are reasonably sensitive toward others. They recognize anguish, despair, disappointment, anger, joy, and contentment in people's faces, actions, and tone of voice. They can usually detect true meanings of people's words and deeds. They rarely, if ever, attempt to impose their values on others or insist that others be mirror images of them. Rather, they accept, as part of people's uniqueness, their differences, desires, and preferences. In short, they believe that people should be allowed to live their lives as they see fit, as long as doing so is not harmful to anyone.

Respectful people know how to talk to others, regardless of their feelings toward them. They know when it is appropriate to ask questions, say nothing, offer help, back away, or express genuine delight. In short, because they are wise, they seem to know when and how to say and do the right things.

Physicians with good bedside manners, other professionals whose conduct says, "You are a valued client," and close friends and relatives whose actions show genuine interest in each other are people whose respectful attitude is reflected in their deeds.

Since being respectful is a key requirement of wisdom, let

me recommend an exercise to help you become aware of actions that say, "I respect you." Write at the top of a sheet of paper, "Actions that Reflect Respect." Then, write down all the respectful behaviors that *you* feel comfortable exhibiting.

Here are a few that you might want to incorporate in your list:

> Ask for what you want, rather than demand it. And be cordial when making requests; "please" and "thank you" make people feel appreciated.

> Consider other ways to *show* people that you appreciate their efforts and that you view them as special. These ways are based on your knowledge of them as people. The more individualized your show of appreciation is, the more it is valued.

> Promise only what you can fulfill and fulfill the promises you make. Promises create expectations, which, when unfulfilled, cause greater disappointments than if no promises were made.

> Inform people well in advance of changes in plans. This is so they can adjust to their disappointment and make alternate plans.

> Before making important decisions, obtain thoughts and opinions from people those decisions will affect. Failure to do so says, in effect, "Your views have no merit; only what I think counts."

> Get to know people who are important to you—their strengths, weaknesses, aspirations, and idiosyncrasies. The better you know the people you value, the better equipped you are to exercise good judgment in your dealings with them.

> Consider the feelings of people who are important to you, and accept the feelings as valid from their perspective.

To reiterate a running theme in this book, treat people the way you would like to be treated. In part, that means being courteous and thoughtful.

Listen. Really listen.

When you are respectful toward others, you make it easier for them to give you what you want. If that isn't reason enough to be respectful to people, consider the English proverb: *He that respects not is not respected.*

20. When listening, view the person talking to you as the most important person in your life.

How do you know when someone is *really* listening to you? How do you know he is not on a mental trip, thinking of rebuttals to your comments, or distracted for whatever reasons? You know because the person's actions and reactions reflect an attitude that says, in effect, "I'm totally with you. While you are talking to me, you are the most important person in my life."

Admittedly, it is a difficult attitude to adopt. But, considering all the benefits you can gain from doing so, it is worthy of your effort. Try it. The next time someone you value is talking to you, tell yourself: *"Right now, this person is the most important person in my life."* See what happens.

Recently, a deaf student reported the results of adopting this attitude. He told the class, "My hearing hasn't changed since I began to practice this attitude, but my listening has improved substantially." It can for you, too.

This section discusses the rationale for adopting that attitude and gives you the tools to employ it. In the next principle you will see how to "read between the lines," i.e., how to be a sensitive listener and hear what people are saying beyond the words, so you can respond appropriately. Why are two principles devoted to listening? Because it is the single most important requirement for learning about other people, yourself, and the world around you. It is also an essential requirement for responding appropriately to people and to problems.

Why It Pays to Really Listen

Almost everything I know about being a father I learned from our four children. They taught me, each in her and his special way, what they needed and wanted from me. All I had to do was listen—really listen—when they talked to me. When I screened out everything except them and the things they were saying to me, I learned about them as people. I learned about their feelings concerning important issues and about their individual needs and how I could fulfill them. From their responses, and when my listening antenna was working, I learned how well I dealt with them and their problems.

Other parents who also enjoy good relationships with their children, couples whose excellent marriages have withstood the test of time, and outstanding corporate managers who are rated as such by people reporting to them have told me essentially the same thing: listening with their hearts, souls, and brains helps them to discover what it takes to make their important relationships work.

As German poet J. W. von Goethe said, "Who wants to understand the poem must go to the land of poetry; who wishes to understand the poet must go to the poet's land." Listening, real listening, leads to the "poet's land." It tells you what he or she knows, thinks, and feels.

Poor listeners rarely have any idea of what is going on in the "poet's land" because they are too engrossed in their own worlds to be even remotely interested in anyone else's. And, since their listening antennae are functioning poorly, their effectiveness suffers because their actions and decisions are based on insufficient, incomplete, or biased information.

Although parenting, managing, and "spousing" appear to be unrelated activities, I refer to them in this context to make this point: The principles and tools employed by excellent listeners are universal. The same principles and tools enable parents, spouses, and managers to connect both emotionally and intellectually with the people they value.

You can also, if you adopt the attitude that the person talking to you is, during the period you are engaged in conversation, the most important person in your life. To make this attitude work for you, you must actually tell yourself: *there is **nothing** I'd rather be doing than being with this person; there is **nothing** more important right now than this person.* You must do this each time you are talking with someone you value. Why? Because you are attempting to change habits that interfere with your listening effectiveness. And as you know, habits, once they have found a cozy and receptive home, stubbornly resist being dumped by their host. The only way to fight the dogged resistance of any bad habit is to overpower it with good ones.

Three Tools

Three useful tools that will improve your ability to concentrate on a speaker are (1) avoid or minimize external and internal distractions, (2) ask appropriate questions in the right way, and (3) paraphrase to ensure that you understand the speaker's message.

I. AVOID OR MINIMIZE EXTERNAL AND INTERNAL DISTRACTIONS

Avoiding *external* distractions is relatively simple to do. If the situation is an important business meeting, have it in a place away from your office so that you are not tempted to look at your mail, rummage through other stuff on your desk, do other things that also are important, or answer the telephone. Even if it is a personal meeting, find a place that will make it easy for you to give your undivided attention to the person.

Allowing yourself to be distracted by external elements says to the speaker, "You are not as important as all this other stuff I'm attending to." That, I assume, is not the message you want to communicate. If, however, you are expecting an important phone call, simply inform the person at the start of your meeting about it and tell him or her that it is the only call you will take. Such advance warning communicates a respect for the speaker.

Reducing *internal* distractions is more difficult, but it can be done. While others are talking to you, are you thinking of what you want to say? Maybe it's a rebuttal to a particular statement, or you're thinking of the contributions you want to make to the discussion. Regardless of the reason, when you are thinking of what you want to say while another person is talking, you shut off your listening mechanism.

But why, you may ask, do people do that? My suspicion is that they don't trust themselves to think on their feet. Believing they need extra time to formulate their ideas, they get a head start while the speaker is talking. If you share this belief, I can assure you it is unfounded. You don't need the extra time, not usually. If you do, ask for time to think about what you want to say, but don't let your concern divert you from the speaker's message. In short, *trust yourself.* Believe in your brain's ability to formulate thoughts reasonably fast. And if an idea occurs to you while the speaker is talking, note it somewhere and continue to be attentive.

A second internal distraction is to be preoccupied with thoughts other than the speaker's subject. You may have other work to do; you may be anticipating a date or another meeting; maybe you're daydreaming about a well-deserved vacation. All those thoughts may be more engaging than the speaker's subject. But if you allow those distractions to control you, you could be depriving yourself of valuable knowledge. To push away your musings, tell yourself again: *there is nothing I'd rather be doing than listening to this person.* This attitude, assuming it's sincere, will help you concentrate and reduce the frequency and length of your mental side trips.

The third internal distraction is to be turned off by disturbing characteristics of the speaker. You may dislike the speaker's looks, manner of talking, or what he or she says. None of those attributes matter when you are listening. All that's important is the message and what you can gain from it.

"I want to learn all I can from or about this person" is an additional attitude that will motivate you to pay full attention to the speaker, despite the annoyances and diversions. You may wish to do what a friend of mine does when she is required to attend a meeting that either doesn't interest her or that is led by someone she dislikes. Under those conditions she treats listening like a treasure hunt. "When I view this unpleasant requirement as a treasure hunt," she says, "I look for knowledge that will benefit me. After all, the speaker isn't a total dud."

Her attitude helps her to push away all negative thoughts, either about the presenter or the subject, and enables her to focus on her selfish interests. You can do the same by focusing on and looking for potential gems in what people say, rather than fixing on speakers' negative characteristics or indulging your biases.

II. ASK APPROPRIATE QUESTIONS
IN THE RIGHT WAY

The nature of your questions and whether or not you ask questions reveal almost as much about you as your actions. Your questions may, in effect, say, "I care about you"; "I'm sincerely interested"; "I'd like to help." Or they may, in effect, say, "I want to impress you"; "I want to make you feel bad"; "I want to place you on the defensive." The message that comes across depends on your attitude, i.e., your state of mind, which is generally affected by what you tell yourself before asking the question.

To see for yourself the effect of attitudes—what you tell yourself—on asking questions, study the following three situations:

> SITUATION I: You are a departmental manager and one of your employees submitted a report to you that was not complete.
>
> ATTITUDE A: "It must have been an oversight."
>
> QUESTIONS: Is there a reason why X and Y are missing from the report? *or*

I'm sure this was an oversight, but this report has X and Y missing. When can you submit the completed report?

ATTITUDE B: "What an incompetent to have submitted an incomplete report."

QUESTIONS: How could you have submitted an incomplete report? *or*
Why did you submit an incomplete report? Have you no pride?

SITUATION II: You received a salary increase that was less than you expected. Being upset, you need to talk to your manager about it.

ATTITUDE A: "I'm not sure why I got less than I expected. But, whatever the reasons, I'd like to know what they are."

QUESTIONS: My salary increase was less than I expected. Could you tell me the reasons? *or*
I was disappointed at my salary increase. What could I have done better that would have made the increase what I hoped for?

ATTITUDE B: "My boss is unfair and unreasonable. He probably doesn't like me."

QUESTIONS: Why would you insult me with the low raise you gave me? *or*
What's the point of working hard if I get a smaller increase than everyone else?

SITUATION III: You were recently promoted to a supervisory position. John, a friend of yours who is now under your supervision, has been coming to work ten to fifteen minutes late every day since you were promoted. Until one of your other employees mentioned it, you were unaware that your friend's behavior was causing a morale problem in the department.

ATTITUDE A: "John isn't aware that his actions are disrupting the department. I've got to tell him so nobody thinks I'm playing favorites."

QUESTIONS: It has come to my attention that your coming in late has people upset. They think I'm playing favorites because I haven't said anything to you about it. Are you aware of this difficulty? *or*
Did you know that people in the department think I'm playing favorites because I haven't said anything to you about your coming to work late?

ATTITUDE B: "I'm really angry that John would take advantage of our friendship and come to work late all the time. I've got to let him know that I don't appreciate him doing this to me."

QUESTIONS: What makes you think that just because we're friends I'd give you special privileges? *or*
Are you taking advantage of our friendship by coming in late all the time?

As you can see, when the attitude is positive, the reasons for the questions are to obtain information and to gain understanding. Those questions lead to solutions of whatever problems prompted the questions. However, when the attitude is negative, the questions are accusatory because they assume the person is guilty. Responses to such accusatory questions tend to be defensive.

To ensure that you consistently ask the right questions in the right way, develop the habit of asking yourself, *What's the main purpose of my question? What other purposes do I have in asking this question?* If your responses indicate that your purposes are positive, you are on the right course. Why? Because positive motives will prompt you to ask questions that lead you to knowledge, insights, and solutions to problems. Negative motives, however, such as wanting to make people feel bad or wanting to place people on the defensive, will cause you to ask inappropriate questions in inappropriate ways.

Here are some positive motives for asking questions.

I sincerely care.

I need the information.

I want to know so I can understand.

I'm genuinely interested.

I want your help.

I want to stimulate you to think.

I want to stimulate a discussion.

Although asking the right questions in the right way reflects your wisdom, so does not asking questions that might expose a person's weaknesses, cause a person discomfort, or trigger a defensive reaction. For example, suppose a friend took an exam that would, if he passed, lead to a promotion. And you knew he was to get the results within two months from the time he took the exam. Three months have passed and he has said nothing to you. Under those conditions, it is appropriate not to ask whether he heard. Why? Because if he had passed, being a friend, he would have told you. Since he probably did not pass, there is no point in you asking.

Not asking questions when it is appropriate to ask demonstrates a *lack* of wisdom. Consider two examples. First, suppose someone says to you, "Boy, did I have a tough day today." Instead of asking what happened or what made it tough, you say, "That's too bad," and then move on to another topic. Second, suppose someone says to you, "I'm working on an exciting project." You respond, "Good luck." In both instances, the responses say, "I'm not interested enough to hear details." Or, more to the point, "I'm not interested in the things that are important to you."

Before leaving this discussion, let me offer you one important two-part "do not" principle concerning "why" questions. First, do not ask "why" questions concerning emotions. Questions such as "Why do you feel that way?" "Why are you upset?" "Why are you so angry?" are likely to engender a response like "I don't know, I just am," or a response that is clearly defensive, such as "If I knew I'd tell you." The reason for such responses is that emotions, being nonrational, are difficult, if not impossible, to explain in rational terms.

Since we aren't necessarily able or willing to analyze our emotions, you would get a better response if you made your "why" questions into "what" questions. Suppose, for example, you want to know why someone you work with is angry with you. Asking "Why are you angry at me?" is less likely to get an honest response than "What did I do to anger you?" or "What did I do to tick you off?" Similarly, "Why are you upset?" is less likely to get an honest response than "What happened to cause your upset?" or simply, "What upset you?"

"What" questions are not as threatening as "why" questions, since they relate to experiences people feel comfortable talking about. When you ask someone what happened to cause whatever reaction you're inquiring about, he is willing to relate the experience. When he does, you learn the reason for his reaction. In short, you can find out the "why" of a particular emotion via the back door with a "what" question.

The second part of this "do not" principle concerning "why" questions is do not ask "why" questions that place people on the defensive, e.g., "Why did you submit an incomplete report?" "Why did you miss the deadline?" "Why are you so inconsiderate?" The only appropriate "why" questions are those that are genuine requests for information or explanations. For example: "Why can't we get together earlier?" or "Why are we using vendor X instead of Y?" As a rule, however, it safer to avoid "why" questions.

III. PARAPHRASE TO ENSURE
THAT YOU UNDERSTAND
THE SPEAKER'S MESSAGE

"If I understand you correctly, you're saying _____. Is that right?" "Would an example of what you're saying be _____?" "What I hear you saying is _____. Correct?" "Are you saying, _____?"

Those are all examples of how paraphrases could be introduced. The words don't really matter as long as they are your words and sincerely convey the spirit of an interested listener, which is: I want to make sure I fully understand what you are saying, so let me tell you what I am hearing and you tell me if it is correct.

Using all three tools for making the speaker the most important person in your life while he or she is talking will doubtlessly sharpen your listening. However, to improve it even more, you also need to be aware of what people are "saying" nonverbally and learn to respond appropriately to those hidden messages. Those are the objectives of the next principle.

21. Acknowledge emotions
before dealing rationally with issues.

The Nature of Two-Part Verbal Messages

People generally do not fully express what they think, feel, or want from others. Rather, they couch their emotions in rational terms. Listen carefully to people talk and you will often hear two messages—one rational and the other emotional—rolled into one sentence. The rational part of the message is conveyed by the words themselves, but the emotional part is usually expressed in ways other than words. Consider the following statements and the two messages each conveys:

"Do I *have* to go to the meeting today?"
Rational Part: Just tell me, either yes or no, if my presence at this meeting is required.
Emotional Part: I'd rather not go to the meeting.

"You're in charge; I'll do it the way *you* want."
Rational Part: I'll do whatever you want me to do, since you're the boss.
Emotional Part: I have some ideas about how this ought to be done. Although I will abide by your wishes, I disagree with the approach and would like an opportunity to offer my recommendations.

"Are you working late *again* tonight?"
Rational Part: Just tell me, yes or no, if you will be coming home late.
Emotional Part: I'm really upset [angry, disappointed] that you've been working late as much as you have. I hope you're not going to disappoint me again.

"You're probably too busy to get together with me."
Rational Part: Knowing how busy you are, I don't expect you to put time aside for me.
Emotional Part: I would really like to spend some time with you. But I don't want to ask for fear you will turn me down.

"I had a really rough day."
Rational Part: The day was more difficult than usual.
Emotional Part: I'm dying to tell you of the hell I had to go through today.

"What do I have to do around here to get recognition?"
Rational Part: Tell me what acts one has to perform to be appreciated.
Emotional Part: I've been working hard, doing what I think is a good job, but I get the feeling nobody cares. To put it bluntly, I feel I'm being taken for granted.

"I wonder if I'm really capable of handling this project."
Rational Part: Reassure me that I can handle this project.

Emotional Part: I'd like to talk with you about some doubts
I have concerning my abilities to handle this project.

Although the emotional part of each two-part message is hidden, to the speaker it is far more important than the rational or verbal part. The hidden message says, in effect, "There is much more to what I'm saying than my words convey. I hope you are perceptive enough to realize that these words are only a prelude to a story I'd really like to tell you. But you have to invite me to relate the story. Your invitation will tell me that you care enough to listen. Without your sincere invitation, I can't be sure you can be trusted with my feelings."

Why, you may ask, don't we say what we mean? Why do we tend to couch our emotions in rational terms? The answer to both questions is that our emotions are like nerves. Being delicate and vulnerable, these nerves require protection from insensitive comments or actions that could be painful. By couching our true feelings in "safe" rational statements that do not expose our vulnerabilities, we test the sensitivity of the person to whom we are talking.

Consider, for example, the statement "I had a really rough day." To pass the sensitivity test of this two-part verbal message, the receiver would have to *sincerely* ask something like "What made it tough?" or "Do you want to talk about it?" If, on the other hand, the person to whom this statement was made disregarded the emotion and said, "That's too bad" or "Well, some days are like that," that response says, in effect, "I'm really not interested in hearing the details of your rough day." Those rational responses tell the person who had the rough day that he better not expose his nerves to this person, since doing so can only cause him pain.

Sending two-part messages is wise, since doing so avoids unnecessary pain from insensitive people, but it is equally wise to recognize when others are doing the same and, when appropriate, to invite them to reveal their feelings. Why bother extending such an invitation? There are two reasons. First, it's an effective way of getting to know people you value. And second, the consequence of disregarding those people's emotions is that you are certain to offend them and risk missing out on vital information.

How to Invite Elaborations

For your invitations to be effective, you must do two things. First, you must convey a genuine caring attitude. You can do this by acknowledging the emotional element in a two-part statement, and allowing the other person to talk about his or her pressing concerns. Second, when the emotions are defused, and the person seems more responsive to reason, address the rational part of the message and deal with the problem at that level.

Although it doesn't matter what words you use to acknowledge emotions, the *spirit* of what you say must be: "I hear what you're *really* saying and I invite you to elaborate." Let's see how acknowledgments of three different statements serve as invitations to elaborate. For each suggested acknowledgment ask yourself, "If *I* made the statement, would I view each of the suggested acknowledgments as sincere invitations to express my real concerns?"

> STATEMENT: This job just isn't as challenging as it used to be.
> ACKNOWLEDGMENTS: 1. It isn't? What would make it more challenging?
> 2. Has the job changed or has it become too easy?
> 3. What happened to prompt that statement?

> STATEMENT: You're in charge; I'll do it the way *you* want.
> ACKNOWLEDGMENTS: 1. Are you saying you have another way?
> 2. Sounds like you're not pleased with my approach.
> 3. What suggestions do *you* have?

> STATEMENT: I'm not sure I'm capable of handling this.
> ACKNOWLEDGMENTS: 1. What parts of this project are you unsure of?

2. What makes you say that?

3. Are you concerned about your abilities or what?

As you can see, each of those acknowledgments, assuming it is sincere, is an invitation that is difficult to pass up. Implied in each invitation are three messages: (1) I care about you as a person and, therefore, I am receptive to what you have to tell me, (2) it's safe to tell me what's on your mind, and (3) I promise not to violate your trust. When the main objective of the acknowledgment, namely to defuse the emotion, is fulfilled, the person expressing the two-part statement is ready to solve the actual problem that prompted the statement.

How Not to Deal with Two-Part Verbal Messages

Although responding appropriately to two-part verbal messages establishes you as a caring, sensitive listener, you can reinforce people's trust in you by honoring the following three cardinal "do not" rules.

Cardinal Rule One: *Never, ever adversely judge people's emotions or tell them, "I know how you feel."*

Imagine your reactions if any of the following statements were leveled at you: "You shouldn't be upset," "You shouldn't be angry," "You're overreacting," "You shouldn't get excited," "You're too sensitive," or "You have no reason to be depressed." Most people would react defensively to such statements. Why? Because they are insults. Such judgments say, in effect, that there is a right and wrong way of feeling about this situation or experience; your feelings are wrong.

But are they? Since emotions are expressions of each person's uniqueness, and, therefore, not universally right or wrong, they are not subject to judgments. If, for example, something angers or upsets you but doesn't affect me, who is right? Actually, we both are—for ourselves. That's why the question of whose emotional response to a particular situation is right is both irrelevant and inappropriate. The fact is, one of the qualities that distinguishes us from each other is our emotional responses to situations. Judging those responses as wrong is tantamount to saying, "You're not entitled to your individuality." No wonder people are insulted and react defensively when their feelings are adversely judged.

Telling someone, "I know how you feel," after he or she relates an emotionally painful experience, is also likely to engender a defensive response. Although it may make you feel good to say that, it usually does nothing for the person to whom that statement is directed. Worse, it may upset the person.

While you may have had a similar experience, both of you felt the experience differently. Since we all want to believe that our emotions are unique, it is inappropriate to tell another person, "I know how you feel." Nobody knows exactly how anyone else feels. Therefore, it would be more appropriate to say something to the effect that you went through a similar situation, or that you can appreciate how he or she feels.

Cardinal Rule Two: *Do not offer "quick fix" solutions to emotionally related problems.* Admittedly, it is tempting, when people relate problems to us, to tell them what they "should" do, as if we are experts on how to run their lives. Do these responses sound familiar? "If you're having problems with your boss, why don't you look for another job?" "Being depressed is common. You're probably bored. You ought to find a hobby." "You ought to take charge of your life and not allow yourself to be pushed around." "You ought to go to a doctor who will give you some medicine for your stress."

If you haven't heard those exact "Band Aid" remedies, you probably heard others that are, at best, amateurish attempts to help people solve complex problems. Although giving people advice when they are emotionally hurting may make *you* feel better, it rarely provides benefit to the people you want to help. Why? Because they're not ready to take your advice, even if it's sensible. Another reason is that it may be the wrong advice because it is based on insufficient information. Finally, the advice you give them is probably only treating a symptom and, therefore, is not in their best future interest.

You know you're offering quick fixes or giving advice prematurely when the person you're giving it to says things like "Yes, but . . . ," "But you don't understand," or "Yeah, OK," all of which mean, "I'm not interested in your help." Such responses are your cues to stop being inappropriately helpful; to stop being rational.

A dictum expressed by Hal, an outstanding salesman I know, that aptly summarizes this cardinal rule is "Don't attempt to sell your grass seed to people until you know about their lawn."

Cardinal Rule Three: *Do not deal rationally with a two-part message until the person is emotionally ready.* The following three examples demonstrate what can happen when one violates this rule, which is really a variation of rule two.

> HARRY: My opinions have absolutely no value to you, do they?
>
> JEFFREY: Sure they do. *(A more appropriate response might be "What gives you that impression?")*
>
> HARRY: No they don't. If they did, you would find time to discuss them with me.
>
> JEFFREY: OK. Do you want to do that now?
>
> HARRY: Forget it.

> KIMBERLY: I wonder what a person has to do to get some recognition around here.
>
> JENNIFER: Well, first of all you have to consistently— *(Kimberly interrupts because Jennifer's response missed her point. A more appropriate response might be "What prompted that statement?")*
>
> KIMBERLY: Frankly, no matter what I would do or how well I would perform I'd be taken for granted.

JENNIFER: No you wouldn't. You just need to try harder. *(Jennifer's rational statement is premature and, therefore, inappropriate.)*

KIMBERLY: Right.

SHARON: I've had such a rough day, I didn't get a chance to make dinner.

BURT: When do you think dinner will be ready? *("What happened?" would be more appropriate.)*

SHARON: Is that all you care about . . . dinner?

BURT: No. But if you had such a rough day maybe we should go out or order in. *(This rational solution is premature. Sharon isn't ready for this.)*

SHARON: Do whatever you want.

The Nature of Two-Part Nonverbal Messages

Sometimes two-part messages are expressed in actions not accompanied by words. The actions—what you see—are the rational part of the nonverbal message. The emotional part is what you don't see. Here are a few examples of actions that have not been expressed verbally:

Someone who is always friendly toward you suddenly is not.

A normally upbeat, cheerful person has been sullen for the past two days.

A person who usually is calm and controlled loses his temper and yells at you for no reason you know of. This happened the last two times you spoke with him.

Someone who for the past five years has been a generous

contributor to an organization for which you are a fund raiser failed to send in his yearly contribution.

Each of those actions reveals part of the story. To find out the rest of it, you'd have to show you care enough to have noticed the unusual behavior and *invite* the person to tell you what those actions mean.

How to Invite Elaborations

Any out-of-the-ordinary behaviors, i.e., those that are out of character for a person, cause us to wonder what is behind them. It stands to reason that the person won't tell you unless you show a sincere interest by extending an invitation that says, in effect, "I am aware of a sudden change in your behavior and I care enough to know what it is—if you want to tell me." This invitation, known as a "perception check," is evidence that you noticed the change and want to help in whatever way the person will let you.

A salesman named Joe normally calls on a particular client once every two weeks and is well received whenever he makes that call. On two consecutive calls the client did not have time to see him. This was Joe's perception check when he phoned the client after the second rejection: "I'm puzzled, Tim; maybe you can help me. The last couple of times I came by, you didn't have time to see me. That's never happened before and I wonder if I've done anything to offend you."

This question opened the door to a dialogue that resulted in a resolution of the problem. As it turned out, Tim was angry with the company, not Joe, because its customer-service department failed to handle a crucial problem that Tim had. Unable to reach Joe for his help, Tim showed his anger toward the company by ignoring Joe.

Let's consider possible perception checks for three of the incidents described earlier.

> INCIDENT: Someone who is always friendly toward you suddenly is not.

PERCEPTION CHECK: Did I do anything to warrant your sudden coldness toward me?

INCIDENT: A normally upbeat person seemed sullen the past two days.

PERCEPTION CHECK: I'm concerned about you. For the past couple days you haven't been yourself. What's going on?

INCIDENT: Someone who has been a generous contributor for the past five years to your organization failed to send in his yearly contribution. Being the chief fund raiser, you decide to do a perception check.

PERCEPTION CHECK: (After the appropriate introduction) We missed your yearly contribution and I wonder whether you could help us out by telling me what, if anything, we did to affect your decision not to contribute this year.

Although the examples describe negative incidents, they could very well involve positive situations. For example, if someone came in to your office looking particularly chipper, a perception check might be, "From the look on your face and the bounce in your walk, I can see that something good happened to you. What was it?"

Be wary of two things regarding perception checks. First, when you refer to behaviors, be specific. General questions such as "What's wrong?" "What's bothering you?" or "How are you doing?" seem to lack the sincerity of questions such as "You walk as though the world were on your shoulders; what's going on?" or "Judging from [refer to the behavior], I think you're trying to tell me something. What is it?" The point is, the person you're addressing needs to know that you care enough to have noticed the specific changes in behaviors and attitudes, be they positive or negative.

Second, if you know what's behind an action, i.e., you know

what's bothering the person, *do not* do a perception check. Rather, tell the person what you know and move forward to solve the problem. You might say, for example, "I know you're angry at me because [whatever specifics you want to relate]. What can we do to get past your anger?" Or "You have every right to be upset. How do you plan to resolve the problem?"

Perception checks are appropriate only when you are uncertain what a particular action means and you are genuinely interested in knowing. If you know what is bothering a person, there is no point in doing a perception check. For example, if you know a person has been fired from his or her job and is depressed, a perception check is inappropriate.

In summary, when you genuinely care about the person who, either verbally or nonverbally, is talking to you, you must view that person as the most important person in your life. That attitude will enable you to listen with your eyes and heart, as well as your ears, and respond appropriately. The person will then consider it safe to take off the mask and tell you what he or she is really thinking and feeling. If you know what the person is really saying, skip the perception check; tell the person what you know and then deal with the problem.

I'd like to end this section with a poem (its author is unknown to me) that captures the spirit of good listening. It's called "Listening for Pain."

> I see it in your eyes and in your face;
> I see it in your walk and hear it in your voice;
> I sense your pain and feel your anger;
> Because I care, I reach out and say softly,
> "Talk to me about what you're feeling."

22. Avoid placing others on the defensive.

Since defensiveness is a reaction to fear, and fear stifles productivity, creativity, and growth, it is wise not to say or do anything that causes people we value to be afraid of or feel threatened by us. Whether a relationship is marketing or personal based, you can be sure that *the stronger the relationship, the less defensive both people are with each other. And the weaker the relationship, the more defensive both people are with each other.*

If you did the exercise for Principle 2, you have already proven both those statements to yourself. However, if you didn't do that exercise, you will find it useful to do a variation of it now: Picture two of your closest friends and write their names on a blank sheet of paper. On a scale of 1 to 10 (with 10 being high), rate them in terms of how defensive you are with each one, and write those ratings beside their names. Next, picture two people you have to deal with, but would prefer not to be around—people you wish you didn't have to talk to but must for whatever reasons. Write down their names and your ratings of how defensive you are with them.

The reason why you are not defensive, or are at worst mildly defensive, with your closest friends is that you trust them. You know they would not say or do anything to deliberately cause you discomfort. But because you fear the reactions of the other two people you pictured, you are highly defensive with them.

All this leads to the following conclusion: *To gain trust from people you value, do not say or do anything that is likely to cause them to be defensive with you.*

Although many people are by nature defensive and will react accordingly at the slightest provocation, most people's defensiveness is learned. They have learned from experience what and how much they can say to whom. They have learned who is trustworthy and who is not. Understandably, their experiences trigger such defensive thoughts as:

> If I'm not careful of what I say, my words will come back to haunt me, just as they did last time when I said what was really on my mind.

> If I offer an unpopular opinion, will that jeopardize my relationship with him (or her)?

I hate playing guessing games, never knowing what's right and what's wrong. I think I better play it safe and do exactly what's expected of me, nothing more.

It's safer just to go along than to disagree.

If I disagree, will that cause me grief?

I hate having to defend every statement I make. It's better to say nothing.

Last time I offered a suggestion he got angry at me; I'm not going to fall into that trap again.

Knowing that trust is a basic requirement of a healthy and strong relationship, wise managers make a conscious effort not to say or do anything that causes others to squirm, sputter, lie, feel guilty, or feel threatened in any way. Provoking others to be defensive weakens the foundation of any relationship and often creates communication barriers. By avoiding the defensive-producing actions discussed in this section, you will gain people's trust and, in doing so, increase their willingness to be forthright and honest with you.

Avoid Adversely Judging Emotions or Opinions

How and what people feel, as well as their opinions about things, characterize them. To threaten their individuality by attacking a particular emotion or questioning its validity is, understandably, offensive and insulting. So is undermining or attacking people's opinions.

Since emotions and opinions are not universally right or wrong, judging them with statements such as "You're wrong" or "I disagree with you" are likely to engender defensive responses. You would be wiser to employ the tools of acknowledging emotions discussed in the previous section.

With regard to opinions that differ from yours, you might

also say such things as "You're entitled to your opinion, but the way I see it, _____," "That's interesting, but let me tell you how I view the situation," or "Based on my experience, I have a different perspective. I'd like your interpretation [then state your experience]." Such responses don't threaten people's dignity and right to see and feel things as they do, nor do they prompt offensive-defensive dialogues. Rather, they encourage discussion and foster opportunities to learn.

In short, if you want people to express their emotions and opinions freely, make sure your responses to them consistently say, in effect, "I respect your right to feel what you feel" and "I respect your right to have an opinion that differs from mine."

Avoid Adversely Judging the Total Person

Many people believe that unless criticism causes pain and makes the person criticized feel bad, guilty, or stupid it is ineffective. Aside from being unfounded, that belief leads to personal judgments that trigger defensiveness, which, of course, delays or prevents resolution of problems.

Four common characteristics of such judgments are:

1. *any* statement beginning with "You" or "You are," followed by a negative comment. (To chastise the total person for a single act is unreasonable.)

2. *any* statement beginning with "You aren't," "You don't," or "You didn't." (Negative statements about others' actions that begin with "You" are typically viewed as personal attacks.)

3. *any* generalization such as "You never _____" or "You always _____," which is intended to strengthen one's position but actually weakens it. (People can usually find an exception to those generalizations.)

4. *any* negative label or abstract term, such as irresponsible, lazy, unwise, incompetent, and bad attitude in reference

to an action that offends your sense of propriety. (Negative labels, no matter how you package them, are offensive. Also, they typically are too vague to be of value.)

To see for yourself the corrosive effect of adversely judging people as people, pretend you are on the receiving end of a statement that falls into each of the four categories. Then, ask yourself, "How would I react if someone said this to me?" For categories 1 and 4, for example, you might imagine your reaction to someone saying to you, "You are so inconsiderate." For category 2 imagine your reaction if someone said, "You aren't carrying your weight on this project." For category 3 imagine how you would respond to "You never listen to me."

Avoid Asking Accusatory-Type Questions

When is a question not a question? When it is an adverse judgment in disguise. The objective of such a "question" is to undermine the person to whom it is directed. As you might expect, people almost invariably respond defensively to such questions. These are a few examples of accusatory questions:

"Why do you feel that you are better than the rest of us?"
"When will you grow up?"
"Why do you have such a bad attitude?"
"Why don't you ever listen to me?"
"How many times have I said _____?"
"Hasn't anybody told you what the rules are?"
"Where were *you* when I made the announcement?"
"How can you be so thoughtless?"

A major characteristic of these "questions" is that no response to them is acceptable, since they are actually indictments disguised as questions. For example, if you were to say to someone, "Why do you have such a bad attitude?" would any explanation the person offered be acceptable to you? Of course not; the only objective of such a "question" is to make the person to whom it is directed feel lousy.

Avoid Asking Trap Questions

Trap questions are called "gotcha questions" or "have-you-stopped-beating-your-mother-yet questions." Either a positive or negative response traps the person to whom it is directed and places him or her in a no-win defensive situation. Consider in the two examples that follow how each question is dealt with when answered both with a yes and a no:

Example I

QUESTIONER: You mean you never learned how to do this?
RESPONDER: Well, actually I did, but I forgot.
QUESTIONER: You sure did; it's like you never learned it.

GOTCHA

QUESTIONER: You mean you never learned how to do this?
RESPONDER: No, I didn't.
QUESTIONER: I can't believe it. I can't believe you didn't ask to learn this.

GOTCHA

Example II

QUESTIONER: Do you know you just contradicted yourself?
RESPONDER: Yes I do.
QUESTIONER: Why would you do that?

GOTCHA

QUESTIONER: Do you know you just contradicted yourself?
RESPONDER: No, I didn't realize it.
QUESTIONER: Well, you did.

GOTCHA

To convince yourself further of the nastiness of trap questions, employ the above procedure with the following six "questions":

> "Do you know you did this wrong?"
> "Are you aware of your insensitivity?"
> "Has it ever occurred to you that _____?"
> "Is this analysis your best effort?"
> "Are you aware that you interrupted me?"
> "You don't believe me, do you?"

Two qualities of trap questions are (1) they begin with "Do you know" (or some variation of it) and are followed by an adverse judgment regardless of the answer, and (2) they are questions to which the questioner knows the answer. Regardless of their form, your trap questions say to the person you are addressing that your intentions are less than honorable.

Avoid Making a Person Feel Guilty

Making a person feel guilty may get you what you want, but the resentment it creates could harm the relationship. Some effective guilt-creating statements refer to actions of a past "offense." Consider the following guilt-producing beginnings:

> "If you hadn't done [or said] _____"
> "If you had only done [or said] _____"
> "You shouldn't have _____"
> "You should have _____"

Those kinds of statements practically beg for defensive reactions, since they say, in effect, *I want you to feel bad.*

Another way of making people feel guilty is to impose "Shoulds." Such statements say, in effect, *You have an obligation to do this; if you don't you are less than a good person.* You can just feel the guilt building up in someone when you say, "You should put in more time on this project," "We haven't seen Sharon and Ed for so long; you should invite them for dinner," or "I don't understand how you could not offer your help. After all, she's your friend."

Another way of making people feel guilty is to agree to help them when they ask for a favor, but accompanying the agreement with a statement such as "I'll do it but it will cause me difficulties" or "OK. I'll help you out but it's time I can't really spare." That's called "giving with strings attached" and is not genuine giving.

While not adversely judging emotions and opinions, not adversely judging people, not asking accusatory-type questions, not asking trap questions, and not making others feel guilty will minimize your unintentional inclinations to place people on the defensive, to help yourself further, consider the following two suggestions.

SUGGESTION ONE

1. Whenever someone responds defensively to you, ask yourself, "What did I just do to cause that defensive reaction?"

2. Whenever someone says or does something that causes *you* to be defensive, ask yourself, "What did that person do to cause that reaction from me?"

Since awareness is the beginning of change, your answers to those questions will prompt you to avoid such actions in the future.

SUGGESTION TWO

Whenever you are inclined to say something that is negative and, therefore, could trigger a defensive reaction, ask yourself, "What's the point of my comment? What will I gain by saying what I'm about to say?" Those questions will reduce your emotional impulse and set you on a rational track. Asking myself, "What's the point?" (which is my abbreviated version of the two questions) has saved me from many potentially dangerous situations. It will help you also. Try it.

23. Make your criticisms helpful.

Each time I conduct a seminar or class discussion on making criticism helpful, I begin by asking, "Would you please raise your hand if you are reluctant or find it difficult to criticize others?" Invariably, between two-thirds and three-fourths of the participants confess to this difficulty. Although they offer many reasons, their explanations tend to fall into three categories: (1) They don't want to offend or antagonize people, (2) they fear reprisals, and (3) they fear some other, less painful, negative personal consequence. All three concerns are based on the assumption that criticism is a bad thing. If you go by the dictionary definition of criticizing, "to find fault" and "to make judgments," the assumption is justifiable.

Before considering an alternative assumption that will lead us to a different conclusion, it is important to distinguish among four words that are often used interchangeably even though they are not the same. The words are *judgment, evaluation, attack,* and *criticism.*

Judgments are assessments based on *subjective* criteria. Statements such as "You are wrong (because it doesn't agree with my views)," "You are right (because I see it the same way)," "This is bad (because I don't like it)," and "This is good (because I like it)" are examples of judgments. When one judges adversely, the intent is to antagonize the other person and make him feel bad. Although the verbal part of an adverse judgment is negative, the *implied* message, which is positive, is "I have another way of viewing or doing this thing I am judging." Since people typically react to the words themselves, not what's implied, adverse judgments, as you know, tend to place the judged on the defensive and often result in offensive-defensive dialogues.

Evaluations are assessments of quality or merit as measured against *objective* criteria or established standards. "Your performance is above average (compared to others in the group)," "Your behavior is inappropriate (because it fails to meet our code of conduct)," and "This report is poor (because the grammar and spelling errors exceed the number of allowable errors)" are all examples of evaluations.

Attacks are verbal assaults intended to injure emotionally and intellectually the object of the attack. They are the kinds of statements we are accustomed to hearing during national and sometimes local elections. Such statements, which frequently take the form of name calling and other character assassinations, are also common during domestic fights where the parties view each other as enemies.

Criticisms will be my focus in this section. The assumption I make in this book is that *criticisms are gifts you give to people you truly care about.* But, for those "gifts" to be well received and useful, you must wrap them attractively and present them properly. You must offer them in ways that cause their recipients to be or perform better. My main desire in this section is to show you how to do this. But first, let's talk more about the nature of criticism and how it differs from adverse judgments.

The Nature of Criticism and What Triggers It

Suppose someone you value said or did something that bothered or maybe even angered you. Or perhaps this person did not say or did not do something he or she should have. Regardless of which situation you choose, you are faced with a problem. Why? Because, as you recall, a problem is a discrepancy between what you want, or believe should be, and what actually is. Although you are upset or angry for having this problem and consider it necessary to criticize the person for causing it, the questions before you are: How do I criticize without feeling guilty? How do I criticize without causing the person to become defensive? and, How do I criticize so the person is grateful rather than resentful?

To answer those questions to your satisfaction requires you to accept the notion that the sole objectives of criticism are positive. Specifically, those objectives are (1) to get the person you are criticizing to see what you see and to realize why it is a problem for you, (2) to show that person what changes will alleviate the problem, and (3) to prevent the behavior that concerns you from recurring. In short, *to qualify as "criticism," your objectives must be motivated by a desire to be helpful and, at the same time, to solve your problems.*

Distinctions Between Criticism and Adverse Judgments

For it to be viewed as a gift, criticism has to be both subtle and instructive. By subtle I mean that the disappointment, anger, upset, or other negative feeling you may be harboring has to be implied. For example, the statement "In the future, if you have a negative comment about my performance, please tell me privately" *implies* that the person being criticized failed to do that, while the verbal message is positive. An adverse judgment concerning the same situation would be "You're so insensitive; how could you embarrass me in front of everybody?" *(The verbal message is, I want you to feel as lousy as you made me feel, while the implied message is, I wish you would criticize my performance privately.)*

For it to be instructive, a criticism has to tell the person *specifically* what you want that you didn't get. If necessary, show the person what you want. For example: "Regarding this report, it would be more effective if the summary of the results were in front rather than in back." In this statement the negative judgment is implied, but the criticism is an instructive gift. An adverse judgment concerning this problem might be "Why would you put the summary of the results in the back when it's the most important part of the report?" *(The verbal message is, You are really stupid.)*

In short, the gift of criticism is a caring statement that, in effect, says such things as:

"I want to help you by giving you my insights on this matter."

"I'm unhappy with this action, but rather than getting angry with you, I'll tell you or show you what I want."

"I care enough to tell you what I see that you may not, and what you can do to change."

An adverse judgment, on the other hand, is a slap in the face.

Since you need the cooperation of the people you criticize to help you solve your problems, treating them as friends is a wise course of action. Hitting them over their heads with a two-by-four and giving them a "piece of your mind," which most people cannot spare, is not.

How to Present Your Gifts Properly

To increase the likelihood that your "gifts" will be well received, the next time you need to criticize someone, plan ahead by first responding to the following four questions:

1. Will your criticism identify, either implicitly or explicitly, the specific problem that concerns you?
    ("I have a problem with _____" or "I'm bothered by _____ [this thing you did or didn't do, said or didn't say]. ")

2. Will you tell the person what *specifically* you want that would enable him or her to resolve your problem or prevent it from recurring?
    ("Next time, I'd appreciate if you would _____.")

3. Will your requests or desires be stated in a way that's helpful?
    (People will be more cooperative if you ask for rather than demand help.)

4. Will you have an agreement on how to prevent the problem from recurring? (This is optional, depending on the problem.)
    ("Could we agree that any expenditure above _____ should be checked with me?")

A positive response to all four questions means you are ready to offer your gifts.

Let's look at some specific examples of how to use those guidelines.

"I wish you would have asked my opinion before you decided on this model. Next time I'd appreciate having a say in the matter."

"I hate negative surprises. Next time, if you're planning to change what we agreed upon, please give me sufficient notice."

"Concerning this report, it would read better if the graphs you discuss were in the report's body rather than in the appendix. Please incorporate the changes and have the report ready for me by [specified date]."

"If you're going to be late, please call me so I can adjust my schedule."

"If you have complaints about anything, please tell *me,* since I'm the only one who can make corrections."

"To prevent spelling errors, please employ the spell check before submitting your reports."

Each of those statements honors the principles suggested by the above four questions. The words you use to criticize are not as important as the intent of your message, which addresses what you *really* want.

Nothing else you say, when your primary objective is to right a perceived wrong, is relevant. It is irrelevant to say all the things that adverse judgments convey, since those statements will not get you closer to what you want. It is also irrelevant to bring up personal issues or past negative events that have little or nothing to do with the act you are concerned with. Realize that what a person has *not* done is far less important than what you want the person to do in the future.

Since the person who has caused you the problem can also help you resolve it, offending that person is unwise. You would be far better off to curb your impulse to say or do anything that can backfire. Being nasty, although tempting, is self-defeating. So is allowing a perceived wrongdoing to fester, since it is kinder to be gently direct than cruelly silent.

I have one caution. Timing, regardless of how effectively stated your criticism may be, is crucial. Criticize only when you are certain the person you're criticizing is receptive. Postpone it, although not for too long, if you sense your words will be wasted. If the person you want to criticize is preoccupied, rushed, in a bad mood, ill, or simply not interested in your gifts and gems of wisdom at the moment you want to share them, choose another, more appropriate time to express your thoughts and feelings.

In conclusion, how receptive others will be to your gifts depends on your tone of voice, as well as your timing. If your tone of voice does not convey a slap on the hand, but rather a desire to get what you want, your chances of getting it will increase.

To help you develop the habit of criticizing properly when it's appropriate, you may wish to keep telling yourself the following. You might even make a sign to serve as a constant reminder.

> Criticizing is a gift of love that should not be withheld from people I care about.

> Tell the person I need to criticize what specifically I want or need.

> Make sure my criticism is helpful.

> I can catch more flies with honey than with vinegar.

> It is kinder to be gently direct than cruelly silent.

I once heard it said that only your good friends will tell you when your deodorant isn't working. But they'll tell you in a kind and gentle way. People who are not your friends, and therefore don't care about you, will simply avoid you.

Be a friend to the people who are important to you; help them be the best they can be with your sensitive, wise criticism.

24. View criticisms you receive as opportunities to learn.

You undoubtedly receive many thoughtless, insensitive adverse judgments that feel like kicks from people disgruntled about something you did, didn't do, said, or didn't say. Such censures may come from a boss, a spouse, a parent, a child, a colleague, a sibling, or any person whose relationship you value. Although these people believe that their cutting words will motivate you to change or to take their advice, their disapproving statements frequently hurt more than help. Their adverse judgments, which they confuse with helpful criticism, do little more than cause you to be defensive. Admittedly, they may not mean to hurt you, but, not knowing better, they do anyway.

So, how do you respond to their insensitive remarks? You might tell a critic, "Hold it. I don't appreciate being talked to that way; would you please rephrase your criticism so it's more palatable to me?" Or you might say, "Would you just tell me what's bothering you without attacking me personally?" Although under certain conditions those may be reasonable responses, in the heat of emotion they could trigger another, even more offensive, adverse judgment.

Another possible response to adverse judgments is to react in your favorite defensive way *(perhaps kick back in whatever way makes you feel good temporarily or maybe disregard completely what the critic has to say by pretending it wasn't said at all)*. Consider the negative consequences of such a reaction. First, you would deprive yourself of potential benefits you could gain from your critic's observations. Second, the critic might counter your defensive reaction with his own defensive response. Why? Because you are ignoring the problem that triggered his "criticism."

For example, suppose your boss, after reading a report you submitted, comments, "This report isn't your best effort, is it?" And you say, "I don't know what you're talking about. I think it's a good report." He replies, "Well, I don't." Obviously, this offensive-defensive dialogue is going nowhere. However, if in response to his "gotcha question" you asked, "What specifically is wrong with this report?" the conversation would move in a positive direction and you would be the beneficiary of your boss's thoughts and recommendations.

If it's true that people stop learning the day they die, many people are well on their way to their final resting place because they respond defensively to most, if not all, adverse judgments. Believing that their critics are enemies, they react accordingly and turn their backs on potential learning opportunities. Ultimately, their reputation of resisting any suggestions and recommendations that differ from theirs catches up with them, and even people who genuinely care won't level with them. Would *you* share your observations, volunteer your help, offer your opinions and insights, or make suggestions and recommendations if your efforts were repeatedly rejected with defensive responses? Of course not.

Cutting off major sources of learning is the price we pay for indiscriminately rejecting potentially helpful criticisms that offend us. Just because a gift is poorly wrapped and insensitively presented doesn't diminish its possible value. Wise people know this. They recognize and pursue learning opportunities, regardless of what form they come in, even if the process is somewhat painful. They consider it unwise to allow relatively unimportant emotional concerns, such as protecting one's ego or perpetuating one's image, to interfere with learning.

A painful experience many years ago taught me the costly consequences of responding defensively to criticism. Jay was a man I met through the PTA at the school our children attended. He was a professional writer who sold numerous articles to such major national publications as *Life*, *Cosmopolitan*, and *Reader's Digest*. Having just completed a piece I wanted to submit for publication, I asked Jay to read it and give me his thoughts on its marketability. Convinced I had a well-written, saleable article, I was eager to hear what I believed would be glowing comments.

When Jay finished reading it, he said, "This is garbage. It's a bunch of general statements and platitudes that would bore readers. The idea is interesting, but that's the only decent thing I can say about it." Pained by his diatribe, I felt like crawling into a hole. There being none available, I thanked him for his time and went home, where I brooded for what seemed like hours. I filed the article and never did anything with it.

Had I viewed his caustic comments as a poorly disguised gift, but a gift nevertheless, I would have asked him what I needed to do to convert this "interesting idea" into a saleable article. But I didn't. Because I was more concerned with my ego and feelings than with learning, I lost a great opportunity.

How many learning opportunities have you allowed to slip past you because you responded defensively to adverse judgments? How many good relationships have you turned your back on because you were offended by poorly worded, but well-intentioned, criticisms? How much good advice (*You should do this or that* or *Next time this happens you should do this or that*) did you pass up because you viewed such implied judgments as a threat to your image? Think about those three questions before you read on.

How You Can Profit from Criticism

To profit from criticism, even if it is worded like an adverse judgment, you must transcend the initial sting that causes your ego to shudder and your defenses to prepare for battle. Realize that once the initial pain wears off, you could be the beneficiary of valuable information, insights, or both. Here is how you can claim those gifts.

First, to minimize the pain and emotional knee-jerk reactions that criticisms trigger, employ the principle discussed earlier: *say nothing for five seconds—nothing.* That silence, painful as it may be, will give you time to consider responses that are more reasonable than the common, impulsive, defensive ones that shut the door to learning.

Second, view criticisms as gestures of goodwill, i.e., gifts of love. After all, who, other than caring people, would have the courage to point out faults and weaknesses that are obvious to others but not to you? Who else but friends would place their desire to help you above their concern for what you think of them? Who else but friends would risk their friendship to be forthright and honest with you?

Third, view the criticism, which, of course, is valid from the critic's perspective, *as an opportunity to learn what the critic sees that you do not.*

Fourth, make a conscious effort to avoid defensive reactions. The five-second principle will help, but it's not enough. You actually must keep reminding yourself not to be defensive.

Don, the successful CEO of a manufacturing company I work with, once said, "I rely on my genuine friends, and other people who care, to teach me things about myself that I am unaware of. I count on their candor to help me improve, both as a manager and as a person. Without their criticism I'd miss out on their valuable insights and knowledge."

Appropriate responses to criticism will enable you to grow and become better than you are. The nature of those responses will vary, depending on whether you agree with the criticism, disagree, or are unsure of what the critic is talking about.

If You Agree with the Criticism . . .

"Yes, you're right" or "I agree" is basically what the critic wants to hear if you agree with the criticism. But your agreement must be followed by an acceptable resolution of the critic's concerns. Three possible resolutions are (1) a genuine promise to correct whatever was criticized, (2) an explanation of why such a promise would be unwise, and (3) an explanation of why a particular promise was not fulfilled. For example:

CRITIC: I don't know how you can get anything done when your desk is such a mess.

RESPONSE I: You're right; I do have to straighten it out. I was planning on doing that as soon as I finish this project.

RESPONSE II: I know it looks messy, but I know where everything is. If I were to straighten things up I'd really be disorganized.

CRITIC: I thought we agreed to meet tonight to discuss our vacation plans.

RESPONSE III: Yes, we did. But something came up at work late this afternoon and I couldn't call you until now. Let's set another date.

There are times when you are rightly accused of hurting or offending someone. If you agree that you indeed committed the offense, accept the responsibility for what you did, apologize, and sincerely promise either to be cautious or to not do it again. "I'm sorry *I* hurt you; I'll be more careful," "I'm sorry *I* upset you; I didn't mean to," or "*I* apologize for letting you down; I'll be more considerate in the future" are acceptable responses. However, it is inappropriate, because it fails to take responsibility for causing the pain, to say, "I'm sorry *you* hurt," "I'm sorry *you're* upset," or "I'm sorry *you* feel I let you down."

To see for yourself the inappropriateness of such responses when you are accused of causing someone pain, imagine you are in your dentist's office and the dentist inadvertently hurts you. You say, "Ow, that hurt." I don't know of any dentist who would respond, "I'm sorry you feel that way." Rather, he or she would sincerely apologize and promise to be more careful.

If You Disagree with the Criticism . . .

You may disagree for one or a combination of three reasons: (1) The criticism is based on incorrect information, (2) you and the critic have different perceptions of the situation, and (3) you and the critic simply had a misunderstanding. Here is an example of 1:

CRITIC: When you leave the office please shut off the lights; they were on all night.

RESPONSE: It's unfortunate the lights were on all night, but when I left the office there were at least three other people here. But I will be sure to shut the lights when I am the last to leave.

In this example, the respondent acknowledges the criticism *(it's unfortunate the lights were on all night)*, introduces a fact not known to the critic *(when I left the office, at least three other people were here)*, and offers a final acknowledgment of the criticism, which expresses appreciation for the importance of the issue *(I will be sure to shut the lights when I am the last to leave)*.

Informing the critic of a fact not previously known to him or her is vital, for it allows the critic to alter the perspective that prompted the criticism. How you introduce the fact is up to you, as long as you first acknowledge the criticism. But the message that must come through is *You have a right to your belief, but let me tell you my side of the story.* Another example:

CRITIC: I thought I asked you to have the report ready for me this morning. How come I don't have it yet?

RESPONSE: It was ready just as I promised, and I gave it to your secretary when I came in today. Do you want me to track it down?

As in the previous example, part of the statement, "It was ready just as I promised," says, in effect, *You have a right to have this report as I promised. Since you don't have it, you have a right to be upset.* The second part of the statement introduces new information that negates the criticism. The third statement, which is an offer of help, reinforces the notion that the person being criticized is responsible.

When you and the critic have different perceptions of something, a constructive exchange could go like this.

CRITIC: You're just not putting in the required effort.

RESPONSE: I thought I was. What am I not doing that I'm supposed to do?

The initial response *(I thought I was)* acknowledges the criticism in a non-argumentative way; it also implies that the respondent does not agree. That acknowledgment and *subtle* disagreement is then followed by a question *(What am I not doing that I'm supposed to?)* that says in effect, *Since you obviously see something I don't, I'm willing to hear your side of the story.*

Note how those concepts are applied in the following two dialogues:

CRITIC: Why do you treat me as if I were stupid?

RESPONSE: I didn't think I was treating you that way, since I consider you brighter than most people around here. What have I done to give you that impression?

CRITIC: You never explained what you wanted from me.

RESPONSE: I thought I did, but let me go over it with you.

Here is a sample dialogue when you and the critic had a misunderstanding:

CRITIC: You were supposed to hand in this report Tuesday; here it is Thursday and I still don't have it.

RESPONSE: I'm sorry for the misunderstanding. I thought you meant next Tuesday. I'll double my efforts and get it to you on Monday.

When disagreements are due to misunderstandings, acknowledging that fact is best accomplished with an apology, followed by an attempt to rectify the problem created by the misunderstanding.

If You Are Unsure of the Critic's Reference . . .

Asking questions is the most direct way to determine what the critic sees and feels that you may not. So, if you are unsure of what the critic is talking about, a simple question will clarify things for you. For example:

CRITIC: You never listen to me.

RESPONSE: What makes you say that? or
What did I do to give you that impression?

CRITIC: I don't see any evidence that you're making progress.

RESPONSE: What specifically are you looking for? or
What do I have to do to prove to you that I am making progress?

Such responses acknowledge the importance of the critic's statements. The message the responses convey is "Since your beliefs and observations are important to me, I want to hear more of what you have to say about the subject and I invite you to tell me." That invitation will prompt the critic to elaborate.

A Summary of Key Points

No matter how poorly worded criticisms are, if they are well intentioned (i.e., they are not name-calling, character-assassinating attacks), you can, if you respond appropriately, benefit from them in at least two ways. First, you can learn about the critics themselves. Their criticisms tell you (1) how they perceive things, i.e., what criteria they use to make judgments; (2) how they actually view you and the things you do or don't do; (3) what they would like you to do differently; and (4) why their suggestions and recommendations would be an improvement over the thing they are criticizing. Second, you can learn about yourself (1) how you and your actions come across to the critics and (2) what you can do to improve.

The following statements will serve as reminders of the major points discussed in this section:

1. All criticism is valid from the critic's perspective. Realizing that, make an effort to determine the nature of that perspective. That is, what does that person see or feel that you may not?

2. Disregard the judgmental aspects of a criticism and address the elements or issues that are most important, i.e., those that can be of greatest benefit to you.

3. Keep your mind open to all viewpoints. Even if they differ from yours, it is an opportunity to learn.

4. Adopt an attitude that says, in effect, "I want to know how I and the things I do or don't do appear to you."

5. All people you value are sources of knowledge and wisdom. Trust yourself to separate useable criticism from that which is not, but don't disregard the message just because it is painful.

6. Avoid taking a defensive position when criticism is leveled at you, since doing so is counterproductive to your primary desire, which is to benefit from criticism.

7. Don't say anything that might cause the person criticizing you to feel guilty or defensive. Responses such as "How could you say such a thing?" or "I can't believe you would say that" (both of which are defensive reactions) could discourage all future criticisms.

25. Use criticisms to augment your managerial wisdom.

Do you recall the first time you heard yourself on tape? The voice, although yours, did not sound like you, did it? You were probably surprised because that voice was either higher, lower, better, or worse than the one you were accustomed to hearing when you spoke.

Similarly, we do not know for certain how we appear in our valued marketing or personal relationships. We may, for example, think we are more or less knowledgeable, understanding, helpful, patient, open-minded, considerate, or generous than we actually are. We may also believe we are fairer and wiser than we actually are. To become better than we really are, those beliefs need to be tested. How else can we know what needs to be changed? How else can we know whether our positive beliefs about ourselves are accurate?

Realizing how important it is to know what customers and employees think, progressive, well-run companies regularly do customer-satisfaction and employee-morale surveys to obtain such information. They use what they learn to make major decisions. Herb, a CEO of one such manufacturing company whose employee turnover rate was negligible and whose profits were respectable, told me, "I *have* to know what our customers and employees think of us as a company. I have to know how they feel about the way we treat them. If I lacked that information, it would be like bowling blindfolded."

Assuming you now view criticism as an opportunity to learn, it would be wise to encourage criticism from people under your influence, that is, people you manage. The approach of encouraging criticism I recommend is one I have successfully employed with corporate clients. Try it and see what it does for you personally, your relationships with the people who report to you, and the productivity of the department you manage.

How to Get Started

You may do this individually or with an entire department of people reporting to you. Assuming it is a department, tell the staff members that the main purpose of this initial meeting is to embark on a plan to improve communication between you and them, regardless of how effective or ineffective it is now. You would be wise to tell them that the success of this plan depends on two requirements: (1) their willingness to be forthright and honest with you and (2) your desire to cooperate with them. Then, promise them that you are committed to do your part by accepting, and not being defensive toward, whatever criticisms they will be expressing. In short, in whatever way you consider appropriate, assure the people participating in this project that your discussions with them will be used *only* in a constructive way.

After your introductory statements, tell them that the first step is for them, as a department, to arrive at a list of specific and reasonable behaviors or characteristics they would expect of *any* excellent manager—one they would willingly extend themselves for. Discuss each statement until all group members agree.

A sales manager I know employed this approach to improve his relationship with his sales force. During the first meeting, they came up with the following reasonable ten behaviors and characteristics they expected of an "Effective Sales Manager and Inspired Leader":

1. An effective sales manager is an objective listener. He listens without preconceived notions, prejudices, and a personal agenda. He listens to learn.

2. An effective sales manager is fair and equitable and does not make emotionally based decisions.

3. An effective sales manager is forthright and operates with integrity. His words and actions are honest and sincere rather than politically expedient or self-oriented.

4. An effective sales manager is a proactive coach who identifies his salespeople's areas of weaknesses and helps them improve. He also is reactive and helps them when *they* ask for it.

5. An effective sales manager creates and encourages a team spirit within the entire department.

6. An effective sales manager follows through on promises and doesn't make promises he cannot keep.

7. An effective sales manager encourages two-way communication so that he can better understand how salespeople achieve their bottom line.

8. An effective sales manager has a consistent, clear game-plan and philosophy for the department and helps each salesperson develop a game-plan for himself.

9. An effective sales manager encourages salespeople to obtain whatever training is necessary for them to become the best they could be. He also regularly reviews accounts with them.

10. An effective sales manager gives sincere "atta boys" when appropriate.

After your group has compiled its own list, tell them they will each receive a printed copy of those statements. When they do, they are to *privately* rate, on a scale of 1 to 10 (with 10 being the best), the consistency with which you exhibit each behavior or characteristic. They are to hold on to those rating sheets until you meet with them individually. Then, (1) promise to set up individual sessions to discuss their ratings and (2) answer questions concerning this process.

If any questions arise, they will be motivated by a desire to be reassured that this is legitimate and there is no hidden agenda. Reassure all questioners that what you told them at the start of the meeting is true: your sole objective is to improve communication between them and you and nothing they say will be held against them.

How to Conduct Individual Meetings

Start off each individual meeting by thanking the employee for his cooperation. Reiterate your promises that nothing he will say will be used against him and that you will be receptive to his criticisms without getting defensive. Realize that if you break either promise you can bid farewell to this self-improvement program. Worse, you will jeopardize your future relationships with your staff.

Next, begin with your lowest-rated behavior. Read it aloud, state your rating on it, and ask the person to tell you what you do or don't do that warrants the rating. While he is talking, listen (take notes as needed). Ask questions or paraphrase so that you are clear about the nature of the criticism, but do not say anything that could be construed as a defensive response. Then, when the person is finished discussing the problems associated with that behavior, suggest possible ways of altering that particular behavior and determine if those would be acceptable.

Follow this procedure for each of the behaviors on which you rated 8 or less. Then, on those where you rated high, read them aloud, and for each ask if this expectation is satisfactorily fulfilled. Since you rated high on them, the answers should be yes.

End the meeting by thanking the employee and promising him to fulfill your end of the agreement by doing everything in your power to work on the low-rated expectations.

By following the above procedure with every employee in your department, you will have a blueprint for being the best and wisest manager you can be. Equally important, your employees will feel valued since they contributed to this achievement.

Follow-up

Approximately six months following the individual meetings, you may wish to have a meeting with each of those same employees to determine their assessment of how you have progressed. Again, encourage them to be candid by honoring your earlier promise not to get defensive.

Realize this is a long-term process in which everyone who participates stands to win.

Other Applications

You can use a variation of this exercise to improve any valued relationship. Suppose, for example, you were interested in improving your relationship with a spouse, a son, a daughter, or a manager of another department. All you would have to do would be to personalize it for the specific situation. For example, you might say, "I would like very much for us to improve our father-son relationship, but I can't do it alone. Let me offer a suggestion. . . ." Then present the plan.

Summary

To augment your wisdom, whether you manage other people or your own life:

1. You need to know what reasonable expectations people you value have of you.

2. You need to know where you stand in terms of those expectations.

3. You must encourage people you value to criticize you without fear of negative consequences.

4. In the interest of improving relationships with people you value, you must be willing to change those behaviors and attitudes that are adversely affecting your relationship.

5. Since you realize that criticism is a gift, you must regularly encourage gift giving from people you value.

26. Silence is the best answer when you have nothing significant to say.

Silence has power and versatility beyond description. When no words can adequately express what or how we feel, silence is the language of choice. Sensitively used, it can console and convey a deep sense of caring, as when a mother silently holds a crying child in her arms. It can be an expression of awe, as when one is spellbound upon seeing Hoover Dam for the first time. Silence can also be cruel and cause confusion, anger, and resentment, as when one person subjects another to "the silent treatment."

Silence says many things, and some of its statements are even contradictory. These are a few of its messages:

I'm angry and want you to suffer the way you made me suffer.

I'm so angry that if I said anything it would not come out right.

I'm too upset to talk.

I choose not to dignify your nasty comments.

I'm touched and can't say anything that would adequately express how I feel.

I approve, which is why I don't think it necessary to say anything.

I disapprove, but I thought you would know that from my actions.

I'm thinking about what you said (or want to say).

I'm listening too intently to say anything.

I've got nothing worthwhile to say.

I don't want to say anything that would break the mood of the moment.

I don't want to say anything to upset you.

I don't want to say anything that might get me into trouble.

I'm disinterested and don't want to encourage you to continue talking.

I don't want to get involved.

I don't want to be the bearer of bad news.

I don't want to reveal what I know.

I don't want to reveal my true feelings.

I don't know.

I'm awed.

I lack confidence to express my thoughts.

Nothing I say will make any difference, so why bother?

Although the meaning that any two people give to silence partly depends on the quality of their relationship, ultimately good judgment dictates when silence is appropriate. One criterion of good judgment is implied in the Danish proverb "Speaking silence is better than senseless speech." However, when silence is intended as punishment or when it is inappropriate, it can be hurtful.

When is speech senseless? When it adds nothing to a conversation, when it does not move a discussion forward, or when it causes pain and triggers defensiveness. Suppose, for example, a person did something that backfired and said to the person who saw it happen, "I can't understand how I could be so stupid." It would be senseless for the other person to say, "Neither can I." Or suppose you dropped something that broke and, out of frustration, you say, "I'm so clumsy." It would be senseless for a person standing next to you to say, "You sure are."

Both those self-deprecations required no response other than silence, since nothing is gained by "adding insult to injury." *It is not wise to slap someone just after he slapped himself.* However, it might be appropriate to soothe the person with such comments as "Oh, it's all right" or "It can happen to any-one," as long as those comments are sincere.

Admittedly, silence is difficult. It requires self-control not to say something, anything, just because there is a pause in con-versation, or just because the other person is expecting a verbal response, or just because we feel we should. Actually, none of those are good enough reasons to talk when silence is appro-priate. To paraphrase a biblical proverb, there is a time to keep silent and a time to speak. Knowing the time to do each is a mark of wisdom.

Other Times When Silence Is Appropriate

In the face of tirades. When a person needs to blow off steam, he or she wants your permission to express those emotions without interruption. Nothing you can say verbally at that moment would appease that person. But by being silent and allowing the person to vent his or her feelings you communi-cate something more profound than any words can convey. Under those conditions your silence says, "I care enough about you to tolerate your tirade, so go ahead and get whatever is bothering you out of your system." It might also say, "I refuse to get into a shouting match with you."

Blowing off steam is a person's expression of anger, but it is not necessarily directed toward you. However, it may very well be a reaction to something you said or did. Actually, it doesn't matter. What does matter is that nothing, other than silence, is appropriate. By viewing such an outburst as a passing storm, you can wait until it passes before getting on with rational issues.

Sometimes letting off steam takes the form of complaints about the world, about oneself, or about other people. Regard-less of their subject and nature, complaints are often expressed by people whose frustrations need to be expressed. These peo-ple are really not interested in what you have to say. Since all they want is a sympathetic ear, silence is your gift to them.

When you are insulted in the presence of others. Silence is also appropriate when you are insulted by a thoughtless comment made in the presence of others—say, for example, when a boss adversely judges you before your peers. Since you do not want to dignify the insult, nor do you want to commit the same boorish act, all you can do is be silent. This is one of those times when asking yourself, "What's the point of saying anything right now?" will help you to maintain silence. Of course you have the right to confront the person privately later, but at this moment nothing you can say would serve your interests.

When the other person is talking about an unrealistic dream. "Someday I will write a book. I have had such an interesting life that people would want to read about it." "When I have enough money I plan to take a trip around the world." Both those statements came from people who I know will never realize their dream. My response to both those people was silence. I let each of them talk about his hopes and dreams uninterrupted. Since there would be no point in saying anything, I simply nodded throughout each one's verbal expression of his someday plans and, when he was through, I said, "Good luck."

When the other person is defensive. There are times when people say and do things that you know are excuses or justifications. Saying anything to undermine their statements will only aggravate their problems. By being silent you allow them to say what they have to say without stripping them of their dignity.

In general:

Silence is an appropriate response to most emotional-based statements.

Silence is appropriate when you, or the person you're talking with, are not ready to be rational.

Silence is appropriate if words will hurt or cause the other person to be embarrassed.

Times When Silence Is Inappropriate

Silence can, of course, be inappropriate. I can think of three conditions when it is insensitive and cruel. Silence is inappropriate

(1) when a person wants and needs a well-deserved verbal pat on the back, (2) when silence is punishment, and (3) when a person is allowed to believe a falsehood about him- or herself.

When a verbal pat on the back is needed. All of us like to be congratulated when we express excitement and pride about an accomplishment. We would like the people with whom we share our excitement to be as happy for us as we are for ourselves. A response of silence when we tell of our good news says, in effect, "I really don't care; I'm not interested in hearing about it." Although the message may indeed be true, it is, nevertheless, insensitive and cruel. A simple "congratulations" or "I'm happy for you" would be more human and, therefore, more appropriate than silence.

When silence is punishment. When you know that someone is angry with you and, instead of telling you the reason, gives you "the silent treatment," what is the person actually saying to you? He could be saying any of the following:

I want you to be as miserable as you made me feel.

I don't want to do anything to resolve our differences.

I want to discontinue our relationship.

I'm too angry to be cordial toward you.

I'm not ready to talk about what's bothering me.

I don't trust you enough to tell you what's bothering me.

I want you to plead for my forgiveness before I'll talk to you.

Given all the possible interpretations of silence-that's-meant-to-punish, "silent treatments" are damaging to a relationship. All they do is cause defensiveness and encourage unwholesome guessing games. Choosing the forthright route is a more appropriate and effective way to handle whatever anger or disappointments may trigger your silence.

When a person is allowed to believe a falsehood about him- or herself. "The cruelest lies are often told in silence," said Robert Louis Stevenson. It is cruel to allow a person to believe he is doing a good job when actually he is not. It is cruel to allow a person to believe that you are pleased with him or her as a person when you are not. It is cruel to allow a person to believe anything that does not reflect your true feelings. Such cruelty is exhibited with inappropriate silence.

Admittedly, a willingness to take risks is needed to tell people the ugly truth about themselves, even if it's done kindly and gently. But isn't doing so considerably kinder than silent adverse judgments? The answer depends on the quality of the relationship. Although many people, like Hans Christian Andersen's "emperor," prefer to be deluded, I believe that most of us would choose to be dealt with truthfully. What do you think?

27. Make it easy for people to give you what you want.

An indisputable fact of life is that people cannot grow emotionally, intellectually, physically, and financially without aid from others. Those who achieve their goals do so primarily because they obtain help and cooperation from people they value. They get people to cooperate willingly by pushing the "right buttons," those that appeal to people's basic needs and wants.

Needs are essentials, while wants are desires. For example, we all *need* to eat, but what we *want* to eat is a matter of individual preference. Although our wants vary and, in part, constitute our uniqueness, we all share the same three basic needs, regardless of our sexual, religious, racial, age, or cultural differences.

> We all need to feel good about ourselves physically, emotionally, and intellectually.

We all need to feel valued, both in terms of what we do and what we are.

We all need help when we implicitly or explicitly request it.

Knowing that *everyone has those same needs,* we can increase our odds of gaining cooperation from people by responding to those needs.

Responding to Others' Needs

You can make it easy for people to give you what you *want* by giving them what they *need.*

When faced with choices of how to use our time or with whom to do business, our final decisions are motivated by our assessments of two factors: the benefits or rewards we anticipate from each option versus the price or negative consequences we envision. The relationship of those two factors as they relate to motivation (i.e., willingness, desire, or enthusiasm toward a particular activity) could be expressed as follows:

Degree of motivation toward "x" =
perceived benefits - perceived price

To put it differently, we do things willingly when we believe that the financial, emotional, intellectual, physical, or other benefits we anticipate outweigh the financial, emotional, intellectual, physical, time, or other costs required. For people to be sufficiently motivated to give you what you want, they have to be convinced that, as a result of extending themselves for you, they can anticipate a payoff greater than the investments required. When payoffs are consistent, people are inclined to do whatever it takes, within reason, to obtain them.

The best payoffs are those that are responsive to people's basic needs, of which there are three. In this next exercise you will consider all the possible ways you can help people meet those needs. In short, using the notebook you employed for the previous exercises, you will think about and write your answers to three questions:

1. What can I say or do that might make people feel good about themselves physically, emotionally, and intellectually?

2. What can I say or do that might make people feel valued, both in terms of what they do and what they are?

3. What do people say or do that *implies* a request for help? That is, what are the symptoms that say, in effect, "Help me"? What might be appropriate responses to all requests for help, whether implicit or explicit?

As you do this exercise, realize that your responses to the questions may overlap, but that's OK.

What can I say or do that might make people feel good about themselves physically, emotionally, and intellectually? Although for the most part people fulfill this need for themselves, you can help in the following ways. Offer appropriate compliments concerning physical appearance. When done tastefully, such compliments are generally taken in the spirit in which they are intended. What other ways can you think of to make people feel good about themselves physically?

Listening to people without passing judgment, asking for their opinions on important matters, and expressing your appreciation for their efforts are three ways that make people feel good about themselves emotionally and intellectually. What other ways can you think of? Engaging people in stimulating discussions and giving them intellectual challenges will also cause them to feel good about themselves intellectually. What other ways can you think of that might make people feel good about themselves in this area?

What can I say or do that might make people feel valued, both in terms of what they do and what they are? We all need to feel important in the eyes of people we respect. Genuine and *specific* compliments fulfill that need, as do meaningful forms of recognition and sincere words of encouragement. How else can you acknowledge the value of people's performance?

Although it is vital to compliment and recognize achievement, as well as encourage people to do their best, it is equally important to value people as people. One way to do that is to get to know them—their likes and dislikes, their idiosyncrasies, and their opinions. Another effective way of showing people that you value them as people is to treat them with respect: listen, be cordial, answer phone calls, be considerate of their time, and fulfill your promises. How else can you demonstrate that you value people as people?

What do people say or do that implies a request for help? What might be appropriate responses to implied or explicit requests for help? Any out-of-the-ordinary behavior, i.e., actions that are out of character, could imply a request for help. In the workplace, an inordinate amount of errors is definitely a cry for help. Complaints of any kind say, in effect, "I've got a problem that I wish you would help me resolve." Constant complaining says, in effect, "I'm hurting badly; I wish you would come to my rescue." What other behaviors are implicit requests for help?

Regardless of whether the request for help is implied or explicit, you would be wise to offer your assistance without making the person feel guilty or inadequate. For example, if particular behaviors are out of character, you might say, "I've noticed X, Y, and Z, which is not like you. Could we talk about what's bothering you?" Or "I know you wouldn't be complaining so much unless this thing was really bothering you. Why don't we talk about it and see what we can do to resolve your concerns?"

By being sensitive to all three of those needs and responding to them, you demonstrate to people that you genuinely care about them. In doing so, you give them good reasons to be responsive to your wants.

Gaining Cooperation

Think of someone you know (whether the relationship is marketing based or personal based) for whom you would do almost anything within reason, not because you feel obligated, but rather because of the kind of person he or she is. When you have this person in mind, write down, in sentence form (not single words), all the characteristics this individual possesses and all the behaviors he or she exhibits that warrant your loyalty. Next, consider each characteristic or behavior and rate yourself on a 1-to-10 scale like the one we've used before. When you've completed that part of the exercise, highlight each of your low scores, i.e., your shortcomings. Finally, taking one shortcoming at a time, make a commitment to yourself to develop that behavior.

Making a commitment is not like an empty New Year's resolution that lasts a few days or weeks. Rather, it is making a conscious effort to institute the change you promised yourself to make. It requires you to think about what you want and to have a plan of action to accomplish your objectives. It requires you to hone the principles and tools discussed in this book, particularly those dealing with building communication bridges between you and people who matter to you. When you consistently live those principles, the shortcoming you are working to overcome will, in time, be replaced by the behaviors you admire.

Then, tackle another shortcoming, and another one after that, until you feel confident that you are consistently doing all you can to foster the loyalty and cooperation that you seek from others. To serve as a constant reminder to make it easy for people to give you what you want, you could make the following sign and hang it next to the others: *What must I give to consistently get what I want?*

A Few Final Words of Wisdom

I believe that most of us have the potential to act wisely much of the time. To do so requires us to activate two related habits that have the power to make wisdom more common than it is. Those habits are to *think about the appropriateness of our actions* and to *think about the consequences of our actions.*

Thinking about our actions in terms of appropriateness and consequences increases the likelihood that our decisions will be right. It also gives us the confidence and courage to dismiss irrational, emotionally based decisions and actions that cause us and others pain, and that also prevent us from getting out of life all the things we deserve. If we are to make our unique, individual world a better place in which to live, we must learn to think about the effects our actions have on ourselves and others, and to exercise reasonable judgment.

When you possess knowledge, you know the right things to say and do. When you possess wisdom, you actually say and do the right things. To transform knowledge into wisdom requires conscious and conscientious effort. The 27 principles discussed in this book, and the tools to use them, will guide you, as they have me, to increase your wisdom. By being a wiser manager, you will, by example, teach others to follow your lead. And, in doing so, you will make a contribution to the betterment of the larger world.

You have my congratulations for your contribution.

Let Me Hear from You

You are invited to write me care of the publisher if you would like help in applying the principles discussed in *Managing with Wisdom*. Please address your request to:

Pelican Publishing Company, Inc.
P.O. Box 3110
Gretna, LA 70054-3110